POEMS SUITABLE TO CURRENT MATERIAL CONDITIONS

FRANK DAVEY

Mansfield Press

Library and Archives Canada Cataloguing in Publication

Davey, Frank, 1940-, author
    Poems suitable to current material conditions / Frank Davey.

ISBN 978-1-77126-053-4 (pbk.)

    I. Title.

PS8557.A63P48 2014   C811'.54   C2014-905716-4

Editor for the press: Stuart Ross
Cover design & typesetting: Stuart Ross

The publication of *Poems Suitable to Current Material Conditions* has
been generously supported by the Canada Council for the Arts and the
Ontario Arts Council.

 Canada Council   Conseil des Arts   ONTARIO ARTS COUNCIL
for the Arts   du Canada   CONSEIL DES ARTS DE L'ONTARIO

Mansfield Press Inc.
25 Mansfield Avenue, Toronto, Ontario, Canada M6J 2A9
Publisher: Denis De Klerck
www.mansfieldpress.net

CONTENTS

1. Poems Suitable

Going Forward / 11

It Is / 12

It's Like, / 14

Time Will Tell / 15

I'm Just Sayin / 17

Recessional Sonnet Concerning Cost-Cutting Poetries / 18

Poetry, Economics, and Anthologies / 19

Not a Poem Because, If, For / 20

Concerns / 22

Net News / 23

I'm Good / 24

It's Imperative / 25

I Was Just Getting Started / 26

Poem Suitable to Some Current Material Conditions / 28

Let Me Be Clear / 29

No Action Is Required of You at this Point in Time / 30

News Briefs / 32

Owning Can Be Wearing / 33

Paying It Forward / 34

Obama's Speech on Poetry Climate Change / 35

This / 38

Calls for Progress / 39

Sarnia Canada Man / 40

That's What I'm All About / 41

Developing Headlines / 42

This Is How / 43

Yes I Did / 44

Openers / 45

You and Me / 46

Your Poem / 48

Who Knew / 49

Going There / 50

Honestly / 51

In the Moment / 52
Poetry Values / 53
8 Feb. 2014: It's All Over / 54
A Message / 55
Bottom Line / 56
The Campaign for Poetry / 57

2. Lack On!
  1. We Lack All / 63
  2. I Have No / 67
  3. Dearth / 72

3. Risky Propositions
  Propositions Concerning Class, Gender, and Sexuality at a
    Canadian Dog Show / 77
  The Conewango Valley Dog / 79
  The Owen Sound Dog, or Why I Have Not Returned to
    Yugoslavia / 80
  The Canadian National Great Dane / 82
  Some Discursive Addresses of Death / 84
  The Cornwall Dog / 86
  Getting Away / 87
  Atwood, ON / 88
  Canadada Dog, or The Pine Ridge Kennel Club Doggerel Slam / 90
  Dog Prizes / 91
  Propositions from a (Reap)praising Margaret Atwood
    Conference / 93
  Dogs and Ethnicity / 96
  The Other Canadian Canon / 97
  Eleven Reasons Why a Straight Guy Might Have Loved a Lesbian / 99
  Specialty Dog Show, Fall 2002 / 100
  'Covering the Death of Derrida / 101
  Dog Modes / 102
  Jammu, Canadian Studies, New Year's Eve, Greetings / 103

4. Par lui-même

George Bowering par lui-même / 111
View Frank Davey's Poetics / 115
The Letters of Mr. O & Mr. C / 124
Ethical Advice Accumulates / 125

1. POEMS SUITABLE

GOING FORWARD

I plan to write a lot more poems going forward.
I expect to find a lot more new phrases
going forward. In the future I think there will be a lot more poems
going forward. Progress depends on it, depends on so much
going forward. Like time, going forward.
We will even have to imagine the past
going forward. Was it really back there
going forward. Are we really going forward
going forward. Will forward always be in only one direction
going forward. I keep asking those things
but they don't seem to be getting me too much forwarder
going forward. If you tried to write a poem going backward
would you be able to see any better where you were going
going forward.

IT IS

It is what it is.
She is what she is.
They've been what they've been.
It was what it was.

Things'll be what they'll be.
Things were what they were.
They would be what they would be.
They are what they are.

We are what we are.
I yam what I yam.
He'll be what he'll be.
Que sera sera.

Boys will be boys.
Convicts will be convicts.
Diabetics will be diabetics.
Sinners will be sinners.

Enemies will be enemies.
Vegans will be vegans.
Russians will be Russians.
Amy Winehouse has been Amy Winehouse.

Poetry will be poetry.
Lindsay Lohan will be Lindsay Lohan.
Racists will be racists.
Assholes will be assholes.

The laws of physics will be the laws of physics.
Gamekeepers will be gamekeepers.
Stenographers will be stenographers.
The North Pole will be the North Pole.

Tiger Woods will be Tiger Woods.
Money will be money.
Homophobes will be homophobes.
Blood will be blood.

Suicide bombers will be suicide bombers.
Roundheads will be Roundheads.
New Amsterdam will be New Amsterdam.
Poutine will be poutin'.

IT'S LIKE,

What's it like where you are?
What's it like now that the army has arrived?
What's it like with all the shops closed up and the school buildings
      trucked away?
What's it like to have had a leg blown off?
What's it like to eat a grasshopper?
What's it like to find your uncle in bed with your mother?
Do you think someone could write about it?
What's it like on the Channel Islands?
What's Yoko Ono like?
What was it like on the last day at Passchendaele?
What's it like to be a candlemaker?
What's it like to have accidentally had sex with your sister?
What was the stillness like at Appomattox? Is that how you spell it?
What was it like for the pit ponies?
What was it like for you? It was good, eh?
What was it like to be Janis Joplin?
What was it like on a slave ship? Does *National Geo* have it right?
What's it like to be thrown into a fiery furnace? Will anyone remember?
What's it like to have your body eaten by dogs?
What's it like to have sailed on the *Bismarck*? Did they welcome
      you home?
What was it like to have your wife sail off with a hot young prince? What
      was it like to have her back?
What's it like in Saskatoon?
What was it like on Utoya Island? Why do people ask?
What's it like to be a Woolworth heir? Do you have to like horses?
What was Pierre Trudeau really like?
What's it like to be a woman poet in Peoria?
What's it like to discover that your daughter has been hanged?
What's it like to live in Ottawa?
What's Paris like?
What was it like to gouge out your own eyes?

TIME WILL TELL

Time will tell in the strictest confidence.
Time will tell whether the times are postcolonial.
Time will tell whether Lady Gaga was gaga.

Time will tell a worldwide audience.
Time will tell whether it will pardon Paul Claudel.
Time will tell you, off.

Time will tell the persons of the years.
Time will tell whether daylight has been saved.
Time will tell when it has expired.

Time will tell whether it is curved.
Time will tell how *Great Expectations* really concluded.
Time will tell tales on dead men.

Time will tell what's on the other side of heaven.
Time will tell what's outside the box.
Time will tell tales.

Time will tell what happened to Amelia Earhart. Or not.
Time will tell whether there are angels or virgins in the afterlife.
Time will tell whether civilization was a dead end.

Time will tell which Smartie got eaten last.
Time will tell why I watched every episode of *Mary Hartman, Mary Hartman*.
Time will tell all we want to know about terrestrial extinctions.

Time will tell the location of every U-boat.
Time will tell the secret of the baby whisperer.
Time will tell whether your index funds are safe.

Time will tell who put the overalls in Mrs. Murphy's chowder.
Time will tell whether unicorns could have been both graceful
and biological.
Time will tell why the lost chord was never found.

Time will tell whether I should have visited Alexandria.
Time will tell whether poetry can be saved.
Time will tell whether you will find a job or a mission.

Time will tell you to remember listservs.
Time will tell everything about the Sierra Madres.
Time will tell how the creature from the lost lagoon got home.

Time will tell whether history got it right.
Time will tell you a fairy tale.
Time will tell whether he did indeed love her to the end of time.

Time will tell what it did to the river.
Time will tell you when it's time to go.
Time will tell how close her sweet lips were to the phone.

Time will tell whether anyone can be alone.
Time will tell whether timing brought me to you.
Time will tell how long the turkey should have been in the oven.

Time will tell whether the beans got spilled.
Time will tell whether anyone has smelled the coffee.
Time will tell whether anyone is listening.

I'M JUST SAYIN

I'm just sayin that Plato never read Marx.
I'm just sayin that if you wait the dog will lap up his vomit.
I'm just sayin that the headquarters of the Luftwaffe is still a
        handsome building.
I'm just sayin that you could have waited.
I'm just sayin just sayin.

I'm just sayin that the mountain pine beetle may bring a brand-new forest.
I'm just sayin that there can be too many eggs in two baskets.
I'm just sayin that the worst thing about politicians is that they often
        believe in what they're trying to do.
I'm just sayin that countries like Canada may never have a century.
I'm just sayin that heart monitors are overrated.

I'm just sayin that the Hellespont is not exactly the Dardanelles.
I'm just sayin that time has nothing to do with essence.
I'm just sayin that the wine made in the hills of Galilee is not
        necessarily kosher and not necessarily holy.
I'm just sayin that someone put a stitch in mine.
I'm just sayin that when the new leaf is turned over it may already be autumn.

RECESSIONAL SONNET CONCERNING COST-CUTTING POETRIES

To cut costs Canadian poets
have used fewer letters in words (B. Bissett),
smaller letters (b. bissett), fewer
vowels (C. Bök), fewer changes
in pitch (M. Atwood), fewer words
taken from dictionaries (A. Karasick), fewer letter spaces
and smaller letters (bpNichol). They have recycled found lines
or sentences (L. Robertson, J.R. Colombo)
or once-abandoned poems (D. Marlatt)
or have re-used and re-used earlier concepts
(I. Layton, R. Souster, A. Purdy *inter alios*).
Some have used their own alphabets (P. Coupey, bpNichol)
or even made their poems go bare (P. Webb).

POETRY, ECONOMICS, AND ANTHOLOGIES
OR
ANTHOLOGY POEM

It is cheaper to publish some poems by ten poets
in an anthology than to publish ten books
by ten poets.

One anthology requires only one bar code, one web page,
one entry in the publisher's catalogue, one inch
on the chain store's bookshelf.
Ten books—wow, that's a lot of books.

In an anthology it is cheaper
to publish poems that fit a standard page format
than to publish poems that contain drawings, footnotes,
a second page or a dead spider in the margin.

Most anthologies present to the reader
hygienically publishable poems.

It is more profitable for a poet to delete the spider
and charge an anthology very little
to include the poem than to have no poem
in the anthology.

There is dead-spider profit, money profit and anthology-fame profit,
all of which can be money profit.

Poems excluded from an anthology may be lousy poems,
bizarre-looking poems, too-long poems or
expensive poems. Poets should avoid writing such poems.

NOT A POEM, BECAUSE, IF, FOR

1.

It's not a poem because it is short.
It's not a poem because there's nothing in it to take us out of 'opinion.'
It's not a poem because it's too pressing.
It's not a poem because today poetry isn't what's needed.
It's not a poem because it lacks a lot of things that are necessary in
        writing poems.
It's not a poem because it doesn't use any poetic devices.
It's not a poem because you know this old girl ain't poetic at all. She don't
        even flow right.
It's definitely not a poem just because you sat in a café on Main & felt poetic.
Did I say it's not a poem because it doesn't rhyme? I merely observed that
        it doesn't rhyme. I even said it was nice. Chill.

2.

It's not a poem if it doesn't rhyme.
It's not a poem if it won't rhyme.
It's not a poem if it isn't passionate.
It's not a poem if there's not a new way to read it.
It's not a poem if you can paraphrase it.
It's not a poem if it never ends.
It's not a poem if its backbone consists of just quotes.
It's not a poem if it just says.
It's not a poem if I can write it another way.
It's not a poem if it only looks like a poem.
It's not a poem if it's abstract.
It's not a poem if it isn't seen.
It's not a poem if it neither loves the people nor respects the land.
It's not a poem if it's not a poem.

3.

It's not a poem for Robyn.
This is not a real ancient Chinese poem—it's not a poem, for starters.
It's not a poem for other readers.
Lots of reasons. It's not a poem, for one.
It's not a poem, for it has no rhythm.
It's not a poem for children.
It's not a poem for which there are easy answers.
It's not a poem for, about or to Ray.
It's not a poem for everybody.
It's not a poem for the girl I was.
It's not a poem, for me—a poem's a visualization of a mind's attempt to
       find an answer.
Consider it an epigram. It's not a poem, for Chrissake!

CONCERNS

I have concerns about the quality of contemporary book reviewing of poetry.

I worry that many clever poetry reviewers are settling old scores or impressing old friends by trying real hard to be cleverer.

It's only a suspicion, but I have grave concerns that many conscientious reviewers don't know enough about poetry to understand much of what they are reading. What did I say?

It makes me uneasy to read reviewers who diss poems, or praise poems, because they rhyme or don't rhyme. Maybe they are reading just the last words of the lines. Maybe the poem is rhyming somewhere else. Maybe the poem is rhyming somehow else.

It bothers me also when a reviewer writes that certain poems are written beautifully. It reminds me of all the beautiful people I've known who I could never get along with and who never wanted to understand poetry. It reminds me of the pains that have arisen from understandings or misunderstandings—including my misunderstandings—of beauty.

I am distressed when I encounter poetry reviewers who use the word *wrought*. What rot, I mutter. Poets are not blacksmiths. *Wrought* is not an ancient past participle of *write*.

I am pained—well, metaphorically pained—when people win prizes for their poems. 'Poetry is not a 4-H club!' I want to yell. 'Even for bpNichol!'

I am really concerned & so am writing this poem.

NET NEWS

Temperance activists raise bar.
Plight of garment workers to be redressed.
Fate of F-35 up in air.
Youth runs for senate seat.
Blind poet reads between the lines.
Navy wins fleeting victory.
Man finds voice at meeting.
Cook succumbs after found in sauce.
Laundress loses four sheets to the wind.
Tin woodsman files suit.
Homeless man found wanting.
Typesetter finds French letters.
Harper keeps complaining about same old thing.
South Florida tenor sings off key.
Convicted killer left hanging.

I'M GOOD

I'm good. Not all the time
but most of it. I'm usually good to go
and good with lots of stuff. I'm mostly good
with who I am and where we're at.
I'm good with how things are.
I'm good with global warming as long
as it don't get too hot, and I'm good
with oil pipelines as long as they don't spill
anywhere important. I'm good with seal hunts
as long as there's still some left for next time
and I'm good with whales in zoos
as long as we don't hear that they're carrying on
intelligent conversations. And I'm good with porn
especially if the actors carry on intelligent conversations
which most of them don't, but if they do
I'm good with it. Really good. And good to go.

IT'S IMPERATIVE

Have no doubt, everything I'm saying is true.
Make no mistake, our situation is dire.
Take my word, everything possible is being done
to make things better.
Rest assured, together we will find a way.
Be certain, we are on your side, and want everything for you
that you would want for yourselves.
Keep in mind, not everyone out there wants us to succeed.
Don't get me wrong, we'll do nothing
you wouldn't have wanted done yourself.
Be confident, all this will be soon behind us.
Have faith, in the people who have come to help you.
Understand, this is no easy task.
Make no mistake, all will be right going forward.
Rest assured, everything I'm saying is true.

I WAS JUST GETTING STARTED

In the beginning, tweets were messages.
In the beginning, heaven was right here on earth.
In the beginning, we thought we had to write the preface first.

To start with, we could have outsourced our metaphors.
For starters, we didn't know about the god particle.
In the beginning is a long time ago to worry about.

To start with, I hate the way you talk.
I was like just getting going.
I was just getting started and already it was 2012, I mean 2013.

In the beginning, the Japanese worshipped nature.
To start with, I knew that.
In the beginning, however, there were no cinemas.

To start with, we had nearly collided with a nuclear sub.
In the beginning, the shares in Poetry Inc. were rising.
For starters, we weren't sure language could handle it.

To begin with, there were phonemes everywhere.
To begin with, we were very young.
For starters, we had to steal paper.

To start with, we studied Indo-Hittite.
For starters, we each ate an apple.
In the beginning, there seemed to be a lot ahead of us.

At first, there's the inauguration.
To begin with, we could hold a book launch.
For starters, commencement seemed so far away.

Once, everything was silent.
I was just getting started back then.
At first, I thought she was aloof.
In the beginning, one word led to another.

POEM SUITABLE TO SOME CURRENT MATERIAL CONDITIONS

A green poem, full of innocence, naivety, and just a little
political savvy, full of hope in fact
to end political savvy. A poem that prefers
a blue box to a bonfire, a cotton bag
to a plastic car, an apple to a rock garden.
I wrote it while walking to work.
I wrote it while drinking from a coconut.
I wrote it while buying an LED light bulb.
I wrote it by pencil in the margins of a Walmart flyer.
I wrote it during Earth Hour.
I wrote it while digging up my lawn to plant milkweed.
I wrote it by candlelight while disconnected
from the grid by a freak tornado.

It's a poem that will become progressively illegible
unless printed with toxin-free ink on recycled paper, a poem
that translates itself into Sanskrit when carried onto Wall Street,
a poem whose implied reader has a carbon footprint
lower than 10 kg.—others
may find it increasingly difficult to see
unless they are offsetting their excesses.
It's a poem that doesn't want to be roundup ready.
It's a poem that overflows with meaning
when read in a rainforest of at least
5 million square kilometres, or underwater
beside a pristine coral reef, or in orbit
around a blue planet still uncluttered with space junk.

LET ME BE CLEAR

Let me be clear about this poem, although I realize
that no one is trying to stop me
from being clear, but anyway let me.
Let me be clear about this
be clear about this poem and poetry, even though of course
many have theorized that poems
should not be clear at all, that the whole purpose
of poems is to muddy the lens, create
uncertainty, ambiguity, paradoxes—or
should that be paradoxa?—simultaneous truths
and that sort of thing, and I agree
and I want to be clear about that. Poets
should be utterly transparent about their intentions
to create problems, puzzlement, grey
area upon gray area. Let me be clear, that
is what I stand for, being clear about plurisignation
and the image nation and the magi nation—
claritas—or Clara Tas as she was rumoured to be known.
Let me be clear, I don't remember ever having had the pleasure
dear Clara, dear Miss Tas, I miss you and that
is why I want to be as clear as possible
but that's another story or another poem.

NO ACTION IS REQUIRED OF YOU AT THIS POINT IN TIME

At this point in time
—whoops, it's already passed—
at that point in time I was just
starting to write this poem
with or without required action
but now it has gone—
the point, that is, not the poem—
& now I am eight lines in
& at a somewhat different point in time. At this
point in time.

He who hesitates loses the point
in time—in a very short time—
I think that's the lesson.
Or the point
at this point in time.
At that point I was hesitating
hesitating to act.
I was carelessly wondering
about the points,
or how pointy, or pointed, time was.
Taking time out to wonder.
Each point in time has four dimensions
I figured, three
of them spatial and one
temporal, & so there could be several
points in time at the same time? Enough points
for Newton & Leibniz to get calculus
invented—at their points in time? Enough
for Wordsworth to see spots maybe

that were here at this point in time
but not necessarily over there at those spots in time. Or,
'That really hit the spot,'
she once murmured in my ear.
'And it's about time.'

NEWS BRIEFS

Police seek wanted man.
Doomed vessel sinks.
Pope says devil real.
US debt impasse dangerous.
5 shot at Oklahoma celebration.
Pitfalls foreseen in data mining.
Get to know Prince Harry's girlfriend.
Capistrano swallow welcomes spring.
Suicide bomber dies.
Man grabs bear's tongue.
Cyclone leaves chaos in wake.
New hijab rules unveiled.
Disaster causes hardship.
Environment Canada seeks cloud services.
Lost silver mine never found.
Merkel condemns US insult.
Free school raises fees.
Blow for Toronto mayor.
Arson investigators under fire.
Nordic model draws sex workers.

OWNING CAN BE WEARING

I take ownership of this poem. I'm not saying
that I own it, like I would a car
or a condominium, but I am admitting,
confessing, owning up,
to using these words, in this order. I'm agreeing
to be responsible. I'll put my name
at the poem's top or bottom, or on the cover of its book,
not because these words haven't been used
before, they've been used lots, and often
in the same phrases, and some
are getting pretty worn, or being made
to serve double or triple duty, but
I'm willing to own what these words in this poem
do, and to wear them if someone
holds them up in front of me
or tosses them in my face.

PAYING IT FORWARD

Poets pay it forward because
the best poets before them also did and are now
being belatedly read in the present and so
poets pay it forward even though most reviewers
are just paying, or paying back, and most editors
are being paid by owners or lenders or shareholders
to stay in business in the present which makes sense because
bills always come in the present and if you pay your bill
forward you just confuse a computer or a credit-rater
but poets if they are paying attention have to
pay it forward because the best readers may be
far ahead, be still in school or not yet
born, look how far ahead
they were for John Donne or
Emily D., not like the line-up at Timmies
or bridges that still have tollbooths
where you can pay forward
only to the next in line.

OBAMA'S SPEECH ON POETRY CLIMATE CHANGE

Do you remember when that man in the moon
looked over at Earth, how beautiful, breathtaking it was—
a glowing marble of blue oceans? Even he can now see
that the poetry he loved to speak
has been changing
in ways that will have profound impacts
on all human poets.

12 of the longest poems in the history of our language
have been written in the past century. Last year
the automated re-use of words in some areas of poetry
reached record highs and the pool
of words considered unpoetic shrank to the smallest size on record
faster than most sociologists had predicted. These are facts.

Now we know that no single poem event is caused solely by climate change.
Haiku, epigrams, and sapphics, they go back to ancient times.
But we also know that in a world where there are more words being used
than there used to be, all language events are affected by a planet ever
more robotic and garrulous. The fact that most of our poetry books
are a half-inch thinner than a century ago
didn't cause books with titles like *The Alphabet, Draft, Footnotes, Day*
or *Metropolis*, but it certainly contributed
to the shrinking that left large parts of our mightiest canon
feeling small and overshadowed.

The potential impacts go far beyond falling word levels. Here at home
2012 was the most silent year in our history. The plains were parched
by the longest sentence drought in its memory. Visual poems scorched
an area larger than *Leaves of Grass*. Only last week a conceptual poet
in nearby Alberta published a whole book made of 90s.

As a resident, as a father, and as a Poet I'm here to say we need to act.

My plan begins by cutting language pollution,
by changing how we use words, using fewer dirty words,
using more clean words, wasting fewer words
throughout our verbal economy. Today
about 40% of our language pollution comes from our conceptual poets.

But here's the thing: right now, there are no limits to the amount of
          language pollution
those poets can pump into our word stock. None. Zero.
We limit the amount of toxic chemicals like mercury and sulfur and arsenic
in our air or our water, but a poet who I know can still
threaten to dump unlimited amounts of the internet into a poem for free.
That's not right, that's not safe, and it needs to stop.

So today, for the sake of our children, I'm directing our Language
          Protection Agency
to put an end to the limitless dumping of pollution from our
          conceptual poets,
and to complete new pollution standards for both new and existing
conceptual poets. Now, what you'll hear from the special interests
and their allies at *Chicago Review* is that this will kill innovation
and crush the literary economy, and basically end
literary free enterprise as we know it. And the reason I know you'll hear
          those things
is because that's what they said every time
someone sets clear rules and better standards for our sonnets and our
          villanelles
and our children's health. And every time, they've been wrong.

For example, in 1970, when we decided through the Clean Poem Act
to do something about the epigraphs that were choking our anthologies—and,
by the way, most young people here aren't old enough
to remember what it was like, but when I was going to school
in 1979-1980 in Los Angeles,
there were days when the folks couldn't go outside because of all the children

struggling to lift those anthologies. And if their language was spectacular
it was from all the pollution in the air.

But what we've learned from this and foreign books
like *R's Boat, Bardy Google, Eunoia, Flatlands* and other disasters
is that we've got to build smarter, more resilient language infrastructure
that can protect our conversations and communications,
and withstand more powerful epics and even flarf. That means building
stronger semiotic walls, phonemic barriers, hardened image grids,
hardened language systems, hardened word supplies. That means
avoiding visual-poetry-induced droughts that can force a country
to truck in poetry from outside.

That image of the man in the moon
contains all those lyric moments we hold dear—
the laughter of children, a quiet sunset, all the hopes
and dreams of posterity—that's what's at stake.
That's what we're fighting for.

Thank you. God bless you. God bless the Unaltered States of Poetry.

THIS

This is going to be a real game changer.
If you're tired of the game you've been playing
or hunting or following
then this is the one for you. A *ree-al*
game changer. It will change
any game you want, baseball into crokinole
antelope into muskoxen
politics into table tennis—you remember that one
right? Even if you play the poetry game
with this game changer you can convert
villanelles to limericks, free verse
to conceptual verse, Galway Kinnell
to Ron Silliman. This is the one you need
a game changer to change all game changers
don't get stuck in the same old game
this will change the game of bonds to the game
of derivatives, a bear market to a bull
equities into sparkling futures
parlour games into war games
sex games into video games
rupees into bitcoins
pyjama games into arcade games
X-Box into MP3
chess into Red Dead Revolver
it will change the game of thrones
to the game of deck chairs, the game of life
to the game of death, the game of love
to whatever you want, what could be better?—but wait
if you buy our guaranteed game changer in the next five minutes
we will send you our new life changer absolutely free
so don't wait, change everything today
get a leg up on the future, be game not gamey, be protean, mercurial
be way far out ahead of the changing game.

CALLS FOR PROGRESS

Substitutes recommended for religion.
New treatments tested for sex offenders.
Alternatives sought to racism.
New approaches considered for child molesters.
Answers suggested to suicide bombers.
New procedures mooted for terrorism.
Mother hits out against family violence.
New methods investigated for executions.
Solutions required for acid attacks.
New thinking needed for gang rape.
Other means considered for war.

SARNIA CANADA MAN

Sarnia Canada man was deeply afraid he was going to die.
Brother says man is now dead in the historic sense that we knew him.
Chased from his hot tub wearing only bathing suit and towel.
Bullets sped past his wet skin.
I now live with a life sentence, man testifies.
I lie night after night in a sleepless den of despair, he says.
Canadians not used to being shot at, his attorney says,
in a veiled reference to Americans or Syrians.
The bullets whizzed and buzzed past his ears.
Just scaring the hell out of him was worth it, shooter tells the court.
So deeply frightened, so traumatized, man hides behind screen in courtroom.
Man raced down street with bullets striking his neighbours' houses
          ahead of him.
His children had locked the doors of his house.
That's the biggest mistake you'll make, the shooter cried out as the man
          began running.
It was a 9mm semi-automatic handgun, it was a .357 Magnum revolver,
the officer tells the court. Sarnia Canada man continues to suffer,
lives now 'only in the physical context,' brother says. The shooter
carried one gun in a computer case and was wearing combat boots, she says.
Desperate for anonymity the man raced back home to his kids.
Canadian man terrorized, traumatized by smell of water, sight of hot tub.

THAT'S WHAT I'M ALL ABOUT

I'm all about poetry, that's
what I'm all about. Lots
of folk will tell you what
they're about, or all about,
like they're all about cutting costs
or all about reducing the deficit or
all about caring, caring for the elderly
or getting our troops back from Afghanistan,
but you can't really trust them
because they're about other things too
like getting you to believe them, especially
getting you to believe them, but I'm
all about poetry & I don't care
whether you believe me, I'm just all about it.

Now lots of others will tell you that they too
are all about poetry but the zinger is
what is this poetry that they are all about?
They are not all all about the same thing, some
are all about poetry that is all about larks and flowers and some
are all about poetry that is the recycling of words
like *flowers* and *all about*, and some
are all about that stuff that is all about guys reliably carrying
lunchbuckets or all about the idea that you can't
step into the same i.d. or idée twice but I'm
about all these things all in the same poetry, the thing
that I'm all about being all about. And I don't care
if you don't believe me but the others
they are all about caring, all about caring
that you believe them and they'll keep telling you what
they are all about and what poetry is all about. Not me.
I've said what I'm all about.

DEVELOPING HEADLINES

Police probe suspicious children deaths in Alberta.
Suspicious police probe children deaths in Alberta.
Police probe children deaths in suspicious Alberta.
Police probe suspicious deaths in Alberta children.
Police children probe suspicious deaths in Alberta.
Police suspicious probe children deaths in Alberta.
Police probe children deaths suspicious in Alberta.
Police probe suspicious in Alberta children deaths.
Police probe suspicious Alberta in children deaths.
Police probe Alberta in suspicious deaths children.
Police probe deaths in suspicious Alberta children.
Police probe Alberta children in suspicious deaths.
Children police probe in suspicious Alberta deaths.
Children police Alberta in suspicious probe deaths.
Children police deaths in suspicious Alberta probe.
Children police Alberta probe in suspicious deaths.
Children police Alberta deaths in suspicious probe.
Children probe police in suspicious Alberta deaths.
Children probe suspicious police in Alberta deaths.
Children probe suspicious in Alberta police deaths.
Children probe suspicious police deaths in Alberta.
Children probe Alberta in suspicious police deaths.
Children probe suspicious Alberta in police deaths.
Suspicious children probe police in Alberta deaths.
Suspicious children probe Alberta in police deaths.
Suspicious children probe deaths in Alberta police.
Suspicious probe in Alberta police children deaths.
Suspicious probe in Alberta police deaths children.
Suspicious deaths in Alberta police children probe.
Suspicious deaths in Alberta police probe children.
Suspicious probe in Alberta police children deaths.
Police deaths suspicious in Alberta children probe.
Police deaths suspicious in Alberta probe children.
Police deaths suspicious Alberta in children probe.
Police deaths suspicious Alberta in probe children.

THIS IS HOW

This is how we do it.
This is how you lose her again.
This is how you remind me of your mother.
This is how.

This is how intelligent design works.
This is how you kill an attack ad.
This is how you can pass safely on the right.
This is really how.

This is how we play with matches.
This is how diabetes swept the nation.
This is how your brain works.
This is how I feel about buying motorcycles.

This is how I floss.
This is how you make an end-of-the-world movie.
This is how you save the elephant.
This is how you hide dog poo in a green box.

This is how it will start.
This is how a sperm whale sleeps.
This is how not to wash your car's windshield.
This is how it all goes down.

This is how they should have covered the war.
This is how cities would look at night without lights.
This is how you respond to rumours.
This is how strontium decays.

This is how you clip your fingernails in space.
This is how you write a memoir.
This is how he got a free smartphone.
This is how you will die.

YES I DID

Yes I did know her, so to speak.
For a while we were very close, you might say.
We shared a few things, in a way.
We both lived downtown, loosely defined.
Those were pretty good years, you could say.
True, she was quite a gal, so I've heard.
But she taught me a lot, or so I believe.
Her workplace was her own game, so to speak.
I never was much interested, at least not in that way.
Did we drift apart? some would say.
We were quite different, in some ways.
She wanted to tell me more, or that's what I've heard.
Me, I could have gone on indefinitely with what I knew, so I thought.
Do I know what happened?—not really, so to speak.
I don't think much happened, in a way.
Though I do still like her, so I'm told.

OPENERS

Do you know the way to San Jacinto?
Do you know where this road goes?
Do you know how we would get to the nearest hospital?
We'd really like to get to Port aux Basques.
Is there an easier route to Regina?
Do you know where the dog show's being held?
Do you remember Frank Moore?
Do you know why Port Dover doesn't show up on my Garmin?
Do you know why your neighbours here elected such a jerk?
We'd like to find someone we could talk to.
Do you know if this is the way to the garden shop?
Do you know why there were no moose at the moose crossing?
Can you tell us why the anti-war parade was so small?
Do you know why my ex-wife moved?
Hey, we'd love to find a town with a good restaurant.

YOU AND ME

I'll write this poem and you'll write a different kind of poem.
I won't look at your poem when you publish it
and you won't look at mine. I don't understand why
you'd want to read a poem you knew you wouldn't like anyway.
So I'm letting both of us off the hook.

Do we have a deal? I'm letting us
off the hook, the double hook,
although you probably don't like that book either.
Too cold, eh, not enough emotion? Or maybe
not enough respect for traditional narration?

No matter, you didn't have to read it and I
don't have to read what you write, so
I'll write this poem and you go ahead
and write a very different kind of poem
which I won't trouble you by reading.

I'll politely write this poem and you'll write a different kind of poem.
I'll ignore your books and you'll decline to pan mine.
I'll stop my sarcasm about lyric epiphanies and you
you'll stop badmouthing flarf and prose poems and poems about poetics
and poems about language being politics. Maybe.

I'll write this poem and you
you'll write a much different kind of poem
with rhymes at the ends of lines instead of in the middle and I'll forgive you.
I won't say I won't say a word, but I won't write that word, I promise. And you
you'll shut your big traditional yap. Oops, sorry.

I'll write this poem, as I'm doing
knowing that you would sneer if you could see it
so I won't ask you to see it, and in return
I'll pretend that your very sincere poems don't exist
as I wish they didn't, as you wish this poem didn't.

But it does exist. So you go ahead and write
your heartfelt poem, or long adventurous poem,
or sweet self-celebrating poem. I don't mind.
Ce n'est pas grave. Ça m'est égal.
I'll just write this poem.

YOUR POEM

Your poem is very important to us.
Your manuscript is very important to us.
Your book is very important to us.
Your poetics are very important to us.

Here is your prize –
Your poem is very important to us.
Here is your grant –
Your work is very important to us.
Here are your complimentary copies—
Your book is very important to us.
Here are your royalties—
Your welfare is very important to us.

Please check the breaks in your line.
Your poem is very important to us.
Please serve on our jury.
Your reputation is very important to us.
Please attend our awards ceremony.
Your work is very important to us.

Here is your encyclopedia entry.
Your poetics are very important to us.
Here is your tax receipt.
Your manuscripts are very important to us.
Here is our draft of your obituary.
Your memory is very important to us.

WHO KNEW

Madonna would be a Christian name.
Kilroy would be here.
Digitalis would predate computers.
Snafu would be a working word.
Justin Bieber would rescue Miley Cyrus.
Many of our friends would have stock futures.
Cruise control would not prevent shipwrecks.
There would still be down escalators.
Cellphones would be rare in prisons.
Olive oil would set a high standard for chastity.
Many of our friends would want oil futures.
Keyboards would 'replace' the pianola.
Global warming would be local.
Robot Valkyrie would go viral.
Words would become poetry.

GOING THERE

His niece has run off to Thailand
with a rock band, but I'm not
going to go there. I don't like rice or fish
I didn't think she did either
but like I said, I ain't going to go there.
I kinda wish she was in a better place
but she's been having a lot of trouble
with her life, ever since her mother died
it don't much bear thinking about
but what you gonna do, it's not a place
I'd want to be, her mother's now
in a better place, but geez
she's dead. I just can't. I'm
just not gonna go there.

HONESTLY

To be honest with you, I'm writing a poem because
it's the most important thing I can do with my time
right now. To be truthful, not a lot of people
would agree with me, or maybe they would.
But to be really upfront with you—not that I'm not
at other times, it's just that all this should be
a regular thing, honesty, etc. But to be absolutely
transparent about things, poetry is underestimated.
Like Keats said, poetry is truth
& truth beauty, meaning just like Lao Tzu
that the truth in poetry should be self-evident
right there, staring you beautifully in the face
without someone having to suss out what its truth is
so to be truthful I'm not going to tell you
what all this is about, because
honestly dammit, it's a poem.

IN THE MOMENT

This poem is being written in the moment.
I have tried writing poems outside the moment
but that doesn't seem to work, so this one
is being written in the moment, or maybe inside
a series of moments
because now, not just momentarily,
I can hardly remember
that first-line moment from just
moments ago.

Really mindful of that I am working hard
at staying in the moment while writing this poem
& having tons of mindfulness of it. This poem,
its sounds—poem, moment, mindful moment...
It used to be that you could be caught up
in the moment, as if the moment were a hawk
or maybe a vulture, but you don't hear
much about that anymore, just like you don't hear much
about nests of singing birds, so poets have to work now
at being in the moment. There are some people
knocking on my front door, but I think
they are in a different moment so I am trying
to ignore them & their moment
& be really mindful of this poem
& its own moment or moments. This is not the moment
for a sweet hello, this is the moment
for a poem with close attention to syllables, junctures,
punctuation, pitch & phonemes & momentary rimes
if no one minds.

POETRY VALUES

Like most things today
poems need values. Not
just values added
but intrinsic values
built-in values
like the air we breathe, like
temperature values, humidex values
wind chill values.

Values are now a big deal for poems.
It's not that poems didn't have values before
but they were subtle, hidden—
no values but in things I believe
one poet said. There's lots of those—
property values, Blue Book values
core sample values, nutrient
reference values, blood sugar values
body mass values—long poems sure have them.

Today's poem, especially today's 'avant' poem
must declare its values
they must be upfront values
community values, data values, home values
blended values, Quebec values
seasonal values, constant field values
exposure limit values, must openly
oppose racist values, heteronormal values
traditional operating values
stock values, dollar values
colour hex values and

what's a poem without obvious values
when there's so many around.
Values, that is.
What would be the value in that.

8 FEB. 2014: IT'S ALL OVER

The age of gods has ended.
Day has ended.
Life has ended.
Your relationship has ended.
The age of sign-ups has ended.
Cramps after your period have ended.
Your remote session has ended.
Bleach has ended.
Your song has ended.
January has ended.
Summer has ended, but we have not been saved.
We're sorry, but this sweepstakes has ended.
Night has ended for another day.
The golden age of spam comments has ended.
The life of normalcy has ended.
Your remote desktop session has ended.
The market streak has ended.
The trial has ended, but the repercussions linger on.
Another love has ended.
The holiday tax cut rebate has ended.
The beta phase has ended.
The application period for 2013 has ended.
Liability after marriage has ended.
A small war has ended.
Pretend the world has ended.
Communicating risks after exposure has ended.
The journey has ended.

A MESSAGE

I'm going to send you a message
and you're going to get the message
really get the message, good people. Sure
it's a difficult message, you may not
understand it, but you'll get it. Got that?
That's the whole purpose of poetry
to send someone a message, a message
that at least they won't forget getting.
And you'd better get it while the gettin's good.
Got that? Sure, it's tough, a tough message,
and you, you're really gonna get it this time, it's
a message you've got comin' to you,
you've had it comin' for a while.
That's the message.

BOTTOM LINE

The bottom line is not the one to begin with.
The bottom line is the one you hope you will know.
It's the one you hope will be sufficient
so you don't have to re-read the other lines.

Sometimes the bottom line is only
a faded bikini line, and sometimes it's the punchline
and you're the one that's punched,
when you get your eyes too close

to the bottom line.
The bottom line
can be the end of the line.
The right-hand end of the line.

If you spend all your time
thinking about the bottom line
you might be writing a lyric poem,
or imagining your life as a lyric poem

and the bottom line is the one
that will make all the other lines about stuff
you were seeing or doing back then add up
give them new value, make them all

shore up your so-called ruins, and say
in some spectacular way
this poem's
bottomed out, everyone.

THE CAMPAIGN FOR POETRY

If I'm published, I'll make sure greedy insurance companies and replacement writers cannot make a mockery of our poetry markets.

I'll refuse to support a Canada where 24-hour news networks and biased media insiders can defile our megapoems.

I'll work for a Canada where reckless bankers, cabinet ministers and sex workers won't deride multicultural pentameters.

My critics are taking donations from shifty Americans, Bertelsmann board members and illiterate Somali pirates.

I refuse to support a Canada where rich oil companies and socialists can fail to buy poetry books.

My critics are palling around with paper cartels, Japanese whalers, homophobes and Rupert Murdoch yes-women.

I want a Canada where overseas manufacturers and John Metcalf can't misrepresent or corrupt our poetics.

Unlike myself, my critics want a Canada where Hollywood writers and Wall Street insiders can sabotage our language verse.

My readers know that I have faith in our innovation, our medical mythologies, CBC reality TV and shifting the ground of all literatures.

I will not stand for a Canada where Mexican drug companies and illegal New Zealand immigrants can disrupt our sacred award shows.

When I'm published, I'll make sure tree-huggers and tribal warlords cannot stop themselves from reading our book-length poems.

Know this: that my poems will protect our First Nations publishers, our inno-cent young writers' smiles and our right to kill unjust copyright legislation.

My critics are receiving money from Access Copyright opponents, terrorists and crooked lawyers.

I will work for a Canada where right-wing radio propagandists and North Korean dictators can chill out on the Coach House Books website.

My critics are taking donations from Carmine Starnino, Iranian extremists and Chilean mining companies.

Unlike my critics, I support our procedural poets, our heroes of 1812, LGBT parades and our delicious saskatoon pies.

I will not stand for a Canada where professional critics and suicide bombers could demolish a poetry app.

I want a Canada where pot smokers and highly paid lobbyists keep on reading and reading poetry.

Know this: that I believe in our right to use the world's ink, our civil rights, our drivel rights and all basic Saussurean principles.

Unlike myself, my critics want a Canada where corporate executives, unstable nuclear regimes and prosody deniers can thwart our efforts to hold spontaneous literary festivals.

My critics are palling around with Order of Canada wannabes, Sun News columnists and copyright extremists.

My readers know that I have faith in Christian Bök's future, our precious kindergartens and our academic freedom.

I refuse to support a Canada where lyric poets, retired engineers and the spouses of poets can undermine the hard work of our non-referential writers.

When I'm published, I'll make sure overpaid CEOs and corrupt politicians cannot reduce our love for a literary Bible.

My readers know that I believe in our young internet poets, transparent clothing and increasing the public lending right.

I refuse to support a Canada where military-industrial warmongers and internet pornographers can destroy our right to borrow literary models from Asia.

When I'm published, I'll make sure Monsanto cronies and Mexican holidays can't sully our cherished Canadian small presses.

My critics are receiving money from Hollywood insiders, Alberta doctors and overseas writers' agents.

I will work for a Canada where the extinction of species and the salaries of senators cannot sabotage our Canadian poetry nights.

Know this: that I will protect our online publishing, Wreck Beach, our Christmas poetry sales and our hard-working intercultural editors.

My critics prefer to read about government bureaucrats, Washington elitists and Taliban school-burners.

Unlike my critics, I support our hard-reading families, our big book retail stores and our job-printing creators.

I want a Canada where Enbridge board members and backroom dealmakers can't smear the poetics of tomorrow.

I will not stand for a Canada where Iraq-invasion apologists, the spring bear hunt and unprincipled politicians can compromise our right to read our poems to the world.

2. LACK ON!

for Fred Wah and Pauline Butling

1. WE LACK ALL

We lack all courage when we greet each other.
We lack all knowledge of this parting.
If we lack all moral knowledge, we cannot
        know this cither.
What we lack, all too often, is coherence.
But the way we organize now, we lack all of
        these aspects.
And because we lack all these things, some of
        the faithful will weaken and be carried
        along with the times.
You, lonesome human, whoever you are,
        maintain that we lack all experience,
        even when we lack all documentation.
Ever more insulated from danger by our material
        things, we lack all appreciation of the
        eternal thin veneer of civilization.
If we have only some of them, we live less
        meaningfully, and if we lack all these
        things, especially the first two, our life
        is meaningless.
We lack concepts for what our will now is;
        indeed, we lack all data for such
        concepts.
'Now, after the June events, do we lack all
        faith?' the young man asked.
We lack all the elements which would afford
        us an idea of his formation.
We lack either the time, the money, or the
        ability to control the experimental
        conditions—and sometimes we lack all.
We must accept that we are vulnerable to error
        in any matter in which we lack all doubt
        or have not led a meaningful inquiry.
We don't know how to debate, we don't know
        how to argue persuasively (mainly because we

lack all the facts), but we do know that all we
know is correct.
As we are now, we lack all memory / Of what we
were before.
Indeed, that 'grace is sufficient for us' even
when we despair and find that we lack all
goodness.
In our African setting we lack all these things
put together.
Also we lack all insight into the connection
between human growth and the being
of man.
We lack all this in today's world, and nobody
wants that all this gets diminished.
Let us say that from this certain moment we
have this degree of strength, this degree
of vision, this courage, but there are
times we lack all of them.
We perform different mental gymnastics when
we realize we lack all the factors.
We lack all knowledge of the phase associated
with the motion of a system.
With an alien being, we lack all sorts of basic
evidential cues.
That we lack all the desired information is a
result of the historical absence of outcome-
based performance measurement in
medicine.
Here we lack all clues.
All promise to supply what we lack; all are
remedies for a human condition which
Lyotard, citing Lacan and Baudrillard,
posits as intrinsic to subjectivity.
We lack 'all the answers' in so many areas, why
should we feel especially guilty about
not having them on sexuality?

We lack all reasonable evidence for supposing
  that there is anything beyond the
  perceptions and thoughts of individuals.
People are dying because we lack all the
  necessities, and our government seems
  to be happy about it.
That is also the reason why our time has
  become so utterly godless and profane:
  we lack all knowledge of the
  unconscious psyche.
We lack all of those things because of the
  amount of corruption that happens
  inside the government.
We cannot fight an enemy if we lack all the
  skills to win.
This means that we lack all intuition on the
  physics of the very short distances (of
  the order of the Planck length) in which
  spacetime itself has probably 'dissolved.'
We lack all those trees.
We lack all confidence.
We lack all the specifics.
We lack all that.
We lack all power of acting.
Though we lack all power of acting, we have
  the power to consent to act or to
  withhold our consent from acting.
Meanwhile, we lack all those qualities that end
  in I-L-I-T-Y: sustainability,
  deployability, mobility, and
  interoperability.
We lack all these things.
We lack all control.
We lack all archaeological evidence for
  Abraham's existence.

We lack all this in our country, just as we lack a
            skin bank and other synthetic materials.
When we lack all the answers, we choose to
            live by faith.
We have the brains in the system; what we lack
            all too often is the vision and the willingness.
We lack all of that shit.
We lack all control over where we must travel.
Why would we think that we lack ALL flaws?
Worse still, more of us could do it but we lack
            all the proper tools.
We lack all the construction materials.
It is not that we lack all interest in the material
            world.
We lack all but the most preliminary studies.
We lack all the abstractions.
We lack all of the above.
They say we lack all the money.
We lack all evidence and therefore
            understanding.
We lack all of these things, and more.

2. I HAVE NO

I have no tomatoes.
I have no sense.
I have no mouth.
I have no fear.
I have no legs.
I have no words.
I have no joy.
I have no doubt.
I have no regrets.
I have no clue.
I have no self-control.
I have no bananas.
I have no sister.
I have no idea.
I have no life.
I have no affiliation.
I have no money.
I have no visible holds.
I have no opinion.
I have no scars.
I have no job.
I have no options.
I have no Link / Data light.
I have no dog.
I have no witty blog titles.
I have no tribe.
I have no explanation.
I have no friends.
I have no guilt.
I have no lust.
I have no worries.
I have no goals.
I have no need.
I have no Previous Page link.

I have no real friends.
I have no sound.
I have no intention.
I have no water.
I have no disk.
I have no other country.
I have no issues.
I have no tickets.
I have no voice.
I have no audio.
I have no resentment.
I have no say.
I have no photos.
I have no use.
I have no plans.
I have no more answers.
I have no picture.
I have no mix options.
I have no expectations.
I have no Phone / Recent Call icon.
I have no ego.
I have no maternal instinct.
I have no point.
I have no collar.
I have no Delete function.
I have no fancy ebios.
I have no health insurance.
I have no pact.
I have no future.
I have nowhere else.
I have no division.
I have no disk space.
I have no teaching experience.
I have no access.
I have no more dropbox invites.
I have no medicine.

I have no legal mouthpiece.
I have no lunch box.
I have no more kids.
I have no computer skills.
I have no reason.
I have no more tears.
I have no pants.
I have no pretensions.
I have no agenda.
I have no more nuclear secrets.
I have no shame.
I have no icons.
I have no secret bank accounts.
I have no sex drive.
I have no clue tabs.
I have no power.
I have no luck.
I have no feelings.
I have no freedom.
I have no broadband connection.
I have no answer.
I have no one to talk to.
I have no TV picture.
I have no memory.
I have no literary interests.
I have no wysiwyg.
I have no Zen.
I have no scream.
I have no internet connection.
I have no illusions.
I have no faith.
I have no mercy.
I have no self.
I have no magic formula.
I have no ambition.
I have no desire.

I have no skills.
I have no debt.
I have no blogroll tab.
I have no credit.
I have no choice.
I have no DVI tab.
I have no sympathy.
I have no interest.
I have no shorts.
I have no signal-processing toolbox.
I have no Start button.
I have nowhere to go.
I have no wrinkles.
I have no bitter feelings.
I have no cannons.
I have no marketing budget.
I have no respect.
I have no past fertility problems.
I have no name.
I have no closet space.
I have no dial tone.
I have no base band.
I have no proof of income.
I have no allergies.
I have no motivation.
I have no remorse.
I have no written contract.
I have no objection.
I have no special talents.
I have no way.
I have no beef.
I have no experience.
I have no tush.
I have no mother.
I have no damages.
I have no knowledge.

I have no sound device.
I have no service.
I have no athletic ability.
I have no beginning.
I have no major concerns.
I have no data plan.
I have no backups.
I have no wish.

3. DEARTH

There is a dearth of accounting positions.
There is a dearth of excited, committed, well-
        trained clinical investigators in psychiatry.
There is a dearth of updates.
There is a dearth of teachers who contribute selflessly.
There is a dearth of quality young players, not only
        in English football, but among all four
        home nations.
However, it seems there is a dearth of local
        leaders.
There is a dearth of information regarding the
        factors that regulate the activity of
        sympathetic neurons innervating
        identified blood vessels.
There is a dearth of Native American porn.
It is unfortunate that there is a dearth of
        real-world logged data to explore usage
        and problems.
There is a dearth of literature in the area of
        coercion in the administration of
        medication.
There is a dearth of souvenir snow globes in
        Malaga so I won't be able to add to my
        collection.
No, but there is a dearth of opportunities for
        quality teachers due to the present
        reservation system.
There is a dearth of quality, capable and able
        young leaders in the topmost structure
        of the party.
Nevertheless, there is a dearth of systematic
        empirical work on the relationship
        between human rights and trade.
There is a dearth of young villains.

There is a dearth of good engineers.
There is a dearth of reference and scholarly
        books in Bahasa Melayu.
There is a dearth of women comedians.
There is a dearth of such brands in the
        midscale.
There is a dearth of darkness.

3. RISKY PROPOSITIONS

PROPOSITIONS CONCERNING CLASS, GENDER, AND SEXUALITY AT A CANADIAN DOG SHOW

A male dog is called a dog.

Most of the exhibitors are women.

Many of the most serious exhibitors are lesbian, although on average the sexuality of dog show exhibitors reflects Canadian demographics.

A female dog is called a bitch.

The sexuality of judges also follows population norms, although exhibitors joke more often about gay judges than about presumably straight judges, and thus increase their visibility.

Joking about the sexuality of judges follows population norms.

A large-boned female dog is called a doggy bitch, and seldom wins points or prizes.

'Bitch' at dog shows is a neutral term, although where a bitch has a woman owner or handler it can be ambiguously applied.

A delicately structured male dog is called a bitchy dog. It also seldom wins points or prizes.

Successful breeders of male dogs have often bred a prize-winning dog to a doggy bitch.

Some successful breeders are gay or lesbian.

A bitchy dog is often neutered or never permitted to breed.

Many pretty bitches are bred because they have become famous for winning prizes.

You could publish this text in an academic magazine or an arts magazine but not in a dog club magazine.

Although homosexual people have fewer children than heterosexual people, the proportion of homosexual people in the population remains constant.

A bitchy dog is usually all-boy.

Dog show people rarely speak of the concept of queer dogs because this would run counter to the dog show economy.

Many dogs will breed anything.

Some dogs do not like to breed bitches, but this is usually explained by reference to trauma or unfortunate training.

Some dogs try to breed other dogs to show the extent of their dominance.

Some bitches decline to be mounted and bred and so their owners use A.I.

Most dogs are too nervous to breed a bitch except on their own territory, but will try to breed a weaker dog anywhere.

You could not publish this text in a school anthology.

THE CONEWANGO VALLEY DOG

The Conewango Valley Dog Show is held across a narrow road from an
old village cemetery. The dog show grounds are filled with motorhomes
and minivans. The cemetery has large green areas awaiting new burials,
or perhaps expansion of the village. There are potted flowers on each of
the judges tables and on twenty or thirty of the graves. There are signs at
the show reading 'Please clean up after your dog.' There are small
American flags on one or two graves. The dog show officials play a
recording of the national anthem at 8 a.m. Several of the taller stone
monuments date from family competitions in the late 19th century.
Around the show rings, young women sport brightly coloured aprons
as they stand at tables to groom their dogs. Most of the trees in the
cemetery are indigenous except for one flowering rhododendron and a
dozen or more cypresses. Most of the breeds of dogs were created
in Europe or Asia. Some exhibitors are exercising their dogs in the
cemetery because it appears less crowded. The dog show grounds have
poles with electrical outlets every 50 feet and a similar number of water
taps, but the cemetery has only water taps. The cemetery allows a wide
range of decoration, including small gardens, flags, plastic valentine
hearts, and hanging flowerpots. Altering the colour of your dog may
cause its disqualification. One grave features a tie-dyed scarf, similar
to those often seen on small dogs at fashion shows. There are vendors
selling brightly coloured dog flags, dog cushions, dog signs, dog
jewellery, and dog planters. The only sign at the cemetery is the one
at the gate that identifies it as a cemetery. This text has created a possibly
meaningless comparison. Possibly not.

THE OWEN SOUND DOG, OR
WHY I HAVE NOT RETURNED TO YUGOSLAVIA

1. I am not sure it is still Yugoslavia.

2. There isn't that much left to visit.

3. I would rather be at a dog show but I am ashamed to say so.

4. I've always enjoyed myself in Yugoslavia and will feel guilty.

5. My invitation this year is to visit Niš, which is close to Pristina, which is close to Srebica, which phonetically resembles Srebrenica.

6. In Canada I can worry about phonetics.

7. I have a lot of good-natured friends in Serbia, or should I say Yugoslavia, and I will be puzzled when I see them again.

8. I want to go back but I am worried about the meaning of my visit. In Yugoslavia meanings, with the assistance of assorted other heavy weapons, have killed thousands.

9. I will feel guilty if I go and I will feel guilty if I do not go and give support to my friends who I am sure have never wanted to kill anyone in Srebrenica or Srebica.

10. Maybe I would rather feel guilty and be warm beside my pacifist dog.

11. My daughter believes that many of the Kosovo villagers we spent an evening drinking with in 1989 are now dead.

12. I took too much pleasure in watching the Serb police drive their army trucks back and forth outside that bar.

13. I don't like countries in which the 'police' have armoured regiments. I prefer Canada where the police borrow armoured vehicles from the military for special aboriginal moments.

14. Usually I know where the armoured vehicles are likely to be in Canada.

15. On my way to the Owen Sound Dog Show my dog and I were stuck on a narrow highway behind a military truck that was carrying a small tank. We risked our lives to pass it.

16. I wish I could drink some vignac and turksa with Dusko or Ileana. I wish I could stroll again with the schoolchildren over the lawns of Kalemegdan, which cover the dead bodies of a bombarded white city.

17. It would be hard to get about because of the shortages of gasoline.

18. Would I be defying the economic sanctions I support and would the embassy send a car to pick me up at the airport?

19. Can I still remember 'Jugoslavia'?

THE CANADIAN NATIONAL GREAT DANE

1.

The Canadian National Great Dane Show is underway on the lawns of an old motel near Niagara. It's a warm sunny day. The skies are free of clouds and free of planes because three days ago, five hundred kilometres southeast, the World Trade Center towers began vigorously burning. The morning paper has reprinted several Middle Eastern cartoons of George Bush as a whimpering dog, apparently to help increase Canadians' knowledge of 'Arab' politics and views of dogs.

2.

Most of the American-owned entries have arrived despite five-hour delays at the nearby border. Because the motel is old, the swimming pool is overgrown with weeds and is fenced off, and many of the units are rented by Immigration Canada to house newly arrived would-be refugees. Two of these families have been standing under the ringside canopy watching the show most of the morning. The three daughters, in tight grey head scarves, and who weigh much less than most of the Great Danes, sometimes laugh and join in the clapping as the dogs trot in line around the ring.

3.

The people leading each dog are hopeful of winning a rosette and a designation: 'winners dog,' 'best of opposite,' 'best brood bitch,' 'award of merit.' The lawns are brown and dry and increasingly slippery under the dogs' feet. The refugee claimants are hopeful of being designated 'admissible,' and seem delighted by their increasing knowledge of Canadian life. Or maybe delighted by a dog's winning. The owners mist their dogs with water when they come panting from the ring, and sometimes hug them if they have won. The dogs sometimes stand in the shade beside the families. None of the busy exhibitors speak to the refugees. None of the laughing daughters ask, 'Can I pet your dog?'

4.

Soon all the dogs, whether they have won or lost, will go back to their doggy beds and their doggy dinners. But the American dogs will eat late, having had to wait five hours again in their air-conditioned minivans at the border. The refugee families will have a choice of submarines or pizza at the adjacent strip mall.

SOME DISCURSIVE ADDRESSES OF DEATH

Flush the goldfish down the toilet. Bury the cat at the back of the garden.
Leave the carcass of the Christmas turkey in a garbage bag at curbside.
Tall Moorish urns supplied by the Humane Society announce
the ashes of your dogs. Romantic, tragic. A nuisance to dust.
An orientalist embarrassment to your heirs.

48 bodies removed from the *Kursk*.

A suntanned beach. A rutted ski slope. An ash-scattering hike
can be a fashionable excursion. A demographic sifting. An upscale
understanding of an infinitely expanding universe.

Quoth Albert Alligator, '60 billion years and the sun's gonna explode,
killing all mankind.'

Aboriginal bones come rolling
upward at construction sites.
Aboriginals come insisting
the bones be treated as sacred, i.e.
be treated better than living natives.

'Short days ago we lived'
a questionable claim.
Pogo, of course, despaired—'And me so young!'

Do you toss dead mice down the garburator?
Or keep your mother mummified in her bed? Or mummyfied
in your belatedly feminist novel?
Or just on her own fireplace mantle
in the plastic box supplied by the crematorium. Boy
that burns me up, she used to tell you.
You pretended you didn't hear
but now conveniently remember.

84

Death of course has no pride, no dominion, no Loblaws,
no listing on the Bourse though most things in the market
are dead. Comfort food,
like mummy's words, or the pictures
on shrimp cans.

After the World Trade Center Bombing, a cheerful journalist
noted that the event's long-term death effect was neutral—
all were going to die once anyway.

THE CORNWALL DOG

The Cornwall and District Dog Show is being held concurrently with
the 'Earth Summit' in Johannesburg. The canine delegates have been
housed in air-conditioned RV's and house trailers on the lawns
surrounding the show ring. The well-being of dogs increases with the
prosperity of humans. Just as in Johannesburg, each delegate goes
into the ring and performs. The performance is a predictable routine.
There is often applause. If a dog must defecate, a human companion
calls 'Clean up!' and a young human appears with a scoop to protect the
environment.

At Bombay's Juhu Beach I saw a dog with its lower jaw broken at right
angles to its head. It seemed an old injury and the dog otherwise
marginally healthy. It was busily scavenging the way many poor people
do. Some would see the dog as a metaphor for the Third World, but I
assure you it was only a persistent dog. Dogs in the wild will kill their
weaker members to end their suffering. Some would take this as a meta-
phor for the actions of industrialized cultures, but I say the Juhu dog
seemed unthreatened. 'Seemed unthreatened.' Often people remark on
how 'euthanasia' sounds like 'youth in Asia.' 'I say.' At most dog shows
almost all the dogs are youthful.

The Madras Canine Club often holds its show in May. The Goldfields
Dogmor Dog of the Year Show is held in August just outside
Johannesburg. The Juhu dog was showing its adaptability. At Goldfields
'Two dogs cringed with embarrassment when their owners got into a
clawing fight,' wrote Cape Town *Sunday Times* reporter Nicola Katz. Most
of the dogs competing are members of planned litters. The world
population is projected to jump to 8 billion by 2030, delegates are told.
Few humans and few dogs worry about planned breeding. 'The dog show
world is very catty and competitive,' Katz quoted one of the combatants.
Surplus dogs are looked after by animal control or canine rescue services.

GETTING AWAY

Children who *get away* are usually found at neighbours'
unless they live on farms or in forests.
Wayward spouses are often found with lovers.

Teenagers who *get away* are often found living
on downtown city streets or in *shelters for the homeless*.
Dogs that *run away* are sometimes found with lovers.

City dogs that get away are found by the Humane Society
or *concerned citizens*.
Dog show dogs that get away are followed by groups of people
variously shouting *Loose dog! Don't chase him! Stop that dog!*

Don't touch her! yelled the Rottweiler breeder at the Oromocto show
when her young bitch, trailing her leash,
swerved in and out of the terrier ring.
Everyone *stood back*, including the terriers.

My teenage son used to climb out his third-floor window after bedtime
but usually climbed back up before breakfast.

My brindle Great Dane *bolted* out the front door
and *broadsided* a Chevy Nova. The dog was unhurt
and happy to come *back home*. The car was *insured*.

Small children *dart out from between parked cars*.
Older children become *chronic runaways*.
Some breeds have *behaviour problems*.
Some car models are *high risk*.

Most *runaways* believe they can come back when they want to.
Risks at home and away from home are *difficult to calculate*.
Few dogs knowingly run away from *home*.

ATWOOD, ON

Atwood, Ontario, is a Block Parent Community.

At the community centre you can play Lions Bingo every Thursday.

Atwood has an Anglican church and a United church.

Across from the Anglican church is the Village Bee handcrafts.

Atwood, Ontario, has a CIBC Banking Centre and a Muffler World.

The backyards of Atwood border on cornfields and pastures for black and white cows.

The centre of the village is Highway 23, which it straddles for about five blocks.

The Atwood Feed Mill advertises Shur-Gain feeds.

Parked outside the Atwood Pet Foods factory at the south end of the village are eight small trucks. The back of each truck is an open bin of easy-to-wash stainless steel.

At the north end is the Atwood Cheese Factory. It specializes in white cheddar.

On the streets you see very few men because they are mostly inside cars or workshops or pickup trucks.

There will be a Laser Tournament, August 9, 10, & 11.

The funeral home is under tall trees on John Street.

Although only three blocks wide, Atwood is considerably north of Mitchell, Ontario.

The Atwood women have bake sales at the Anglican parish hall.

There is a 4-H club but no Cubs or Brownies.

The east-west streets are named after the apostles.

No McDonald's, no bowling alley, no pool room.

On a map Atwood is nevertheless to the left of Godfrey, Ontario, and much to the left of Metcalf, Ontario.

There is no message to welcome the traveller,
but at both ends of the town a signboard—
'Atwood wishes you a safe journey.'

CANADADA DOG, OR
THE PINE RIDGE KENNEL CLUB DOGGEREL SLAM

The dog 'says' bark or woof or bow-wow, all of which are textual
signifiers for various oral signifiers. The signifier is not the meaning.
'No barking,' barks a spectator. Whatever signification the dog discerns.
There are also raised hackles, fists—body language that matters. There is
the position of the shoulders. The slight leaning of the pasterns. The sig-
nified may not be the meaning. There is desire in woofing. Hwah-hwah,
says—or sighs—the Shar-Pei. There is desire in shouting 'No barking.'
And in typing it here. Saying woof is like crying wolf—there is a woof
but not necessarily a wolf. Wolf-wolf.

'It's only words,' Saussure's student protested or marvelled.

Woof-woof etc-etc. is an oral performance. It has rhythm, self-expression,
authenticity, ambiguity, commitment. It has the cachet of a despised
discourse. Chiens de toutes races. To the uttering dog it is inspired
sound, Dionysian, Eleusian, Parnassian. Excitable speech. Not at all
demotic, nor clean of nose. Both ready-made and infinitely iterable. 'No
barking,' the spectator shouts again. But differently. Language cannot do
justice. A raised eyebrow or leg. The dog does not seek applause. Nor the
spectator. 'Woof-woof-woof.' No barking. Woof-woof. Bark. Wow.

DOG PRIZES

Dog prizes do not resemble literary prizes. Dog prizes regulate the size, shape and style of dogs. They maintain traditional breed standards.

To have your pet win the grand prize at a dog show is not at all like winning a literary prize. To win a dog prize it helps to have a traditional friend on the judging panel. It helps that throughout the year you deliver coffee to judges when you see them sitting at ringside. It helps that you advertise your dog as 'best' in numerous canine magazines.

Literary value is quite different from kennel-club breed standards, even though 'officially recognized' does mean, in doggy language, 'canonical.' The only dogs considered for the grand prize are those that are entered, which leaves a lot of inglorious dogs named Milton languishing at firesides. It helps that you sit with prospective judges and chat about structural problems in your competition. About them not being born the colour they display. About them using illegal substances. Or that you observe sagely and loudly that some move too slowly. That they are well-regarded only in other countries, or in rural communities.

It helps to parade your pet and his trophies through crowds where judges congregate. It helps to go to dog parties. To go to the right shows. To introduce your dog in a purely social tail-wagging way to influential breeders. To talk frequently about good breeding. Literary prizes are less tractable because editors, ex-editors, schoolmates, and envious competitors never sit on judging panels. And when a book is called a dog, it makes prize-winning less likely.

The kennel club, however, forbids your family members from judging your dog. Forbids judges who once sold you a dog. Forbids judges who recently have paid you to exhibit their own dogs. But it does not forbid ex-spouses, or your son's judge girlfriend, or judges whose dogs compete with yours, or judges who you once paid to exhibit your dog, or judges who were once your kennel help. It helps to encourage your kennel help and your children's lovers to become judges. It helps to be a judge yourself and to make a deal with a judge who would also like his dog to win. It is therefore both easier and more difficult to win a dog prize than a literary prize.

PROPOSITIONS FROM A (REAP)PRAISING MARGARET ATWOOD CONFERENCE

1. Opening ceremonies

No one can sound more jaded than Margaret Atwood:
Paul Gessell, *The Ottawa Citizen.*

There are more than 100 registrants from 14 countries:
organizer John Moss, addressing communicants.

Hordes of academics from around the world
descending on Ottawa to dissect every line: Paul Gessell.

For publication, papers should be mailed to Professor Moss:
Tobi Kozakewich, conference assistant.

You don't read them because it would drive you mad:
Margaret Atwood, responding to Gessell.

North is over there: John Moss.

2. Celebrity

Margaret Atwood needs both to affirm and disvalue celebrity:
Lorraine York.

Why do you do this?: Margaret Atwood asking John Moss
about scholars at conferences.

Ikons begin their lives as iconoclasts: Laura Moss
on transnational imagination.

There are 41 metres of Atwood papers in the Fisher deposit:
Robert McGill, Thomas Fisher librarian.

Canadians are balloon puncturers: Margaret Atwood,
prefacing a slide show.

3. *Archive chatter*

An abandoned draft has been abjected: Robert McGill.

An abjected draft becomes a commodity when archived:
someone's notes.

Abandoning & archiving drafts is a mode of self-fashioning:
someone's notes.

The purpose of an archive is
> to lift the veil on a writer's life
> to make money
> to assist critics
> to mislead critics
> to control critics: Robert McGill.

4. *Overhearing*

Writers must own their own privately produced property in order
to participate in a market economy: Renée Hulan.

What is heard is somewhat different from what is said: Barbara Godard.

We know all about her and we do not know her at all: John Moss.

The private is constructed for public suitability: Lorraine York.

It would be your worst nightmare if I had attended your sessions:
Margaret Atwood, still prefacing.

5. Nature

All the characters in *Oryx and Crake* are cyborgs:
Michele Lacombe.

If humans are natural, and naturally produce cyborgs,
are cyborgs natural?: Atwood reader.

Margaret Atwood is a cyborg?: Passing student.

Here I am as half a windmill: Margaret Atwood showing a slide
of two four-year-old girls dressed as one windmill.

6. Destiny

History is written backwards: Coral Howells.

This is me at the Bohemian Embassy, listening
to Sylvia Fricker: Margaret Atwood.

The novel is unsuitable for addressing postnational
posthumanistic culture: Diana Brydon.

You can tell which one's the Queen by the hairdo:
Margaret Atwood.

Love is always inadequate to actual experience:
Tae Yamamoto.

Here I am getting married: Margaret Atwood.

And here I'm reading Tarot cards: Margaret Atwood.

DOGS AND ETHNICITY

Afghan Hound. American Eskimo Dog. Chinese Shar-Pei. English Cocker Spaniel. Irish Wolfhound. Australian Cattle Dog. Argentine Dogo. Or is the multinational Golden Retriever the normative breed? Great Dane. Belgian Lakenois. German Shepherd. French Bulldog. Pomeranian. Tibetan Mastiff. Scottie. Greater Swiss Mountain Dog. Or is the kennel club a universalizing institution?

English Bulldog. Canadian Eskimo Dog. Japanese Spaniel. Norwegian Elkhound. Norwegian Buhund. Deutsche Dogge. Must a real breed breed true? Mexican Hairless. Portuguese Water Dog. Peruvian Inca Orchid. American Bull Terrier. Why are hybrids called mutts? American Staffordshire Terrier. Welsh Terrier. Belgian Shepherd. Disjuncture and difference in the global cultural economy.

Ibizan Hound. Bouvier des Flandres. German Pinscher. Belgian Tervuren. Anatolian Shepherd. Czechoslovakian Wolfdog. Can the in-between be reciprocal? Pembroke Welsh Corgi. Zimbabwean Ridgeback. Chinese Crested. Belgian Malinois. American English Coonhound? Dog breeds build on diversity and energy. American Water Spaniel. Swedish Vallhund. Thai Ridgeback. German Spitz.

English Foxhound. Polish Lowland Sheepdog. Tibetan Spaniel. Bracco Italiano. Caucasian Mountain Dog? Can the subtle Maltese speak? Icelandic Sheepdog. Spinone Italiano. All dog breeds descend from the same ancient female wolf. Irish Water Spaniel. Black Russian Terrier. German Wirehaired Pointer. Discuss the ethics of the territorializing of difference. German Shorthaired Pointer.

Old English Sheepdog. Australian Terrier. Nationalism or colonialism. Irish Red and White Setter. Portuguese Podengo. Cane Corso. Additional readings on diaspora. Scottish Deerhound. American Foxhound. Norwegian Lundehund. Most dog breeds are hybrid creations of nineteenth-century European breeders. Italian Greyhound. Welsh Springer Spaniel. Tibetan Terrier. Finnish Lapphund.

THE OTHER CANADIAN CANON

Journeying & the reruns
Pizza shall destroy mommy
Bar-talk with a geranium
Diamond girl

Dreaming backwardly
I'm a strangler here myself
Under the rips of debt
The first stirring of the breasts
Rude men of the west

The night the dog smelled
They shall inhibit the earth
The double look
The teats of the mighty
God is not a *Tish* inspector

A voice from the lunatic
Nobody owns the mirth
The rubber bride
The bummer book
The wives of the saints

Danby's monsters
The witch's boo
The woman who got it on at Jasper Station
Considers her nays
The smoking facts

The animals in fat country
The dumb foundling
The synergy of slaves
The tush garden

Where is the vice coming from?
Lovers and messier men
West coast tail poems
Running in the family way
The woman next door is poignant

Who has seen the wendigo
Various persons named Kevin whatchamacallit?
What's so big about greed?
Disappearing mood coffee?
No language is new

Spurious
Poses are difficult here
There's a prick with a knife
A drunken clockmaker
She tries her tongue her silvaculture gently inflates

The stubborn posterior of grace
Waiting for Sasquatch
Go to bleep, world
Cry Arafat!

Love when the flights are long
Shake hands with the dingleman
Sunshine kvetches from a little town
Beware of other measures
What we all wrong for

Selling ablutions
Scandalous buddies
Let us compress mythologies

ELEVEN REASONS WHY A STRAIGHT GUY MIGHT HAVE LOVED A LESBIAN

1. He wasn't quite straight, he liked her father.

2. She was mostly a political lesbian.

3. This site, she said later, was under construction.

4. He was one of the jerks who helped turn her.

5. Lesbian isn't a person, it's a position.

6. He believed in social hybridity.

7. He didn't like competing with guys.

8. He imagined threesomes.

9. He feared women who might trap him.

10. Loving is a position.

11. He felt surges of lesbian desire.

SPECIALTY DOG SHOW, FALL 2002

In Iraq, the president is planning his one-candidate election victory. In Florida, judges appointed by the Bush family are looking forward to a prosperous New Year. Here, it's just a dog show. The defeated dogs and exhibitors are leaving the ring. The husband and friends of the winning exhibitor are still jumping up and down clapping and yelling and trying to act surprised. It's a sunny fall day. Some sunbathing dogs and exhibitors are enjoying it so much they haven't raised their heads to look. The winner is grinning, maybe because she was on the club committee that hired the judge. The judge is expressionless, perhaps hoping no one cares that she sold the winner most of her dogs. Even you can speculate. The dog has its ears up, wondering why its master is so agitated when no one else is. Simultaneity is a theory of art. It's not a bad dog, a bit sway-backed, its head slightly too big for its body, some muscles oddly obtrusive. It will limp slightly when it walks from the ring. Some people have said that Saddam and George are not bad presidents. In ten years no one except the winner will remember. The winning dog will be dead. Under a nearby tree the club president is saying to an unhappy idealist, 'Relax, it's only a dog show.' Of course the winner is happy. Jean Chrétien lied about cancelling the GST but, like Saddam, was still delighted to win. In four years some of the dog's sway-backed puppies will be winning shows like this under special or extra-special judges. 'A fine representative of a winner,' says the photographer. Only he can see the image in his viewfinder. 'Why compete?' say some Democrats. Some gymnasts. Third World athletes who are too poor to buy the undetectable steroid. Next week the winner will advertise her win in places where her relationship to the judge is unknown. She is planning more wins. George Bush is gathering Enron money to contest the 2004 election. Jean Chrétien is boasting that he won't increase the GST. Paul Martin is collecting Bay Street money to finance his succession to Jean. Ben Johnson is fantasizing a comeback.

'COVERING THE DEATH OF DERRIDA

(From Aporias, cover)

Would be properly mine. Derrida has repeatedly. Be an appropriate
question. Various ways. The analytic of death. 'My death—is it possible?'
Have and account for. Between singularity and generality. Would be
properly mine. That is the question. The whole of his work. The analytic
of death. A new frontier. How is this question. The apoetical obligation.
Theorizations of death. Must take place. More properly mine. Histories
of death. The trans-national trans-cultural law. A figure of death. An
analytical tour de force. The aporia of 'my death.' Must take place
from now on. Without compromising it. Broached the question. The
corresponding necessity. And yet to respect. And death. One of the
aporetic experiences. Nothing closer. 'My death.' How and by whom.
How this figure. How is this.

DOG MODES

In lyric mode dogs crouch & howl.
Or whine. There may or may not be a moon.
Oh Cynthia, oh chaste Diana
in the Paul Anka dog translation. Or also the familiar
woe, woughooooo, my dinner
has fallen on the thorns of life translation.

In pastoral mode dogs
run around in circles.

In epic mode dogs strut & growl.
Raise tails as personal battle flags.
Then feint & lunge & thrust & parry
also known as the cut & thrust of the canine
question period.

In satiric mode...
Dogs do not have a satiric mode.

In romantic mode dogs
are mostly business, just a minimum
of forepaw play.

For dramatic mode, see lyric.

JAMMU, CANADIAN STUDIES, NEW YEAR'S EVE, GREETINGS

I.

At the university breakfast has not appeared. The chef has had an argument with his sous-chef who is also his wife, & who has retaliated by letting the cooking fires go out. Our Indian colleagues are standing in the pavillion's open courtyard, where breakfast is usually served, each wearing several sweaters & shivering. Except for the women scholars of Bombay, who have stayed home to protest academic politics. Like India, the sweaters are of diverse & conflicting patterns.

We Canadians are in these Kashmiri foothills not to celebrate New Year's but to parse years in Canada. Soldiers with AK-47s stand outside our seminar rooms. Our words have value.

2.

The chef has spent the night in the arms of the sous-chef, who is not his wife, & both have let the cooking fires go out. It is a beautiful cool & misty British Columbia summer morning. Or the chef has slept in, & my hypothermic Indian colleagues are punishing him by making up stories. Even though this is Kashmir, the university buildings are mostly of south Indian design and lack glass in their windows.

Architectural imperialism.
'Colleague' means friendly gesture.

3.

The desk clerk at our Ashoka hotel is selling French champagne for $700 a bottle. Stan Dragland is not tempted, & keeps phoning to try to retrieve his journal, which he sleepily left on the Delhi plane. We pass through a metal detector to enter the lobby. No lack of glass here. Well-tempered crystal corridors connect the hotel's many wings, display us to the surrounding woods. The spiritual sound of Hindi classical muzak.

4.

Our Indian colleagues are staying in the concrete guest bunkers on campus. Abe Rotstein makes sure we have a hotel car to take us the 3 miles to the university. We joke that the 'Government of India' decals on its sides resemble bull's eyes.

'Colleagues' means people who do similar things but most of the things we do aren't.

Bull's eyes.

5.

The cooking staff are living in makeshift tents and lean-tos behind the pavillion. Like my colleagues, I have met & admired the sous-chef. Barefoot young men rush in with bronze pots filled with hot charcoal for us to stand beside. 'White man build big fire stand way back; Indian build small fire stand real close,' my dad used to recite whenever we were camping & he'd decided he wanted to be 'Indian.' In India the only ones who go camping are the poor. Trips of a lifetime. As a child in British Columbia, my dad had owned several books about Indian woodlore. These were different Indians, many of whom also still stand close to small fires. They were not his colleagues.

6.

Breakfast is fried eggs, tomatoes, toast, various curries, & is two
hours late & delicious. The sun is up, our Indian colleagues are standing
in the sunshine on the lawn in front of the pavillion. The ones from
Delhi are plotting to keep the men from Baroda off the executive. We
could have eaten in our hotel but we would have had to pay for the
food. We could have eaten in our hotel but would have had only
ourselves as colleagues.

A lot of Kashmiris find their country unacceptably marginal to India.
Our Indian colleagues from Baroda and Bombay find themselves
marginal to our colleagues from Delhi.

Possible academic paper: 'Collegiality in Kashmir.'

7.

Kashmir's Chief Minister flies to the opening of the conference in his
helicopter. Hundreds of troops secure the university grounds for his
arrival. An international academic conference confers normality on its
host. Each normal day the Jammu newspaper reports three or four bomb
blasts.

Possible academic paper: 'Canadian Studies: a worthy target.'

8.

We all pass through another metal detector to enter the auditorium. On
the stage, the officials garland each other with flowers. The speeches are
short because the Chief Minister wishes to rush to a safer or perhaps
more dangerous place. This is India, or at least is presently India.

I am also on the stage, a garlanded speaker. Some margins are more mainstream than others. 'Globalization,' I say. Are the guns on safety? My mettle has not been detected. 'Postnationalism,' I say. I had a chance to say 'multiculturalism' at a Canadian Studies conference in Sarajevo during the first week of the Bosnian war, but I cancelled.

8.

That evening the Chief Minister hosts in his palace a many-course conference banquet behind three layers of detectors. On our way our government car is stopped by soldiers but the driver is casual about stopping. The soldiers run casually beside us with guns casually levelled. I understand why the Chief Minister prefers his helicopter.

They haul our driver out & march him to the rear of the car. A young Canadian woman colleague who had joined us at the hotel begins shouting & screaming because she thinks they are going to execute him. I no longer want to be her colleague. I think they may execute her because she is shouting & screaming, but I may be projecting. Military roadblocks are a normal part of life in many countries, but are enacted variably.

She implies breathlessly that the rest of us are naive. Our naive driver has produced numerous papers & jumps back in & casually drives us to the next roadblock, where he stops less casually. Tomorrow she will speak about 'natural form & ancient wisdom in Douglas Cardinal's architecture.'

Nostalgia for aboriginal culture can be an amateur critique of capitalism. Or of Canadian collegiality.

Or architectural sentiment.

9.

The buffet dinner presents several spiced meat dishes that I keep
returning to. The Chief Minister is not here. He is somewhere in his
bomb-proof helicopter. But a locally famous elderly cabinet minister
shakes our hands. Our colleagues from Madurai are plotting to put Dr.
Sadat, our Moslem friend from Baroda, on the executive.
Increasingly, I see myself as a meat-hungry Canadian. When we leave
in another government car the streets are empty except for dogs &
government cars & soldiers.

Empty streets are rare in India. The young Canadian woman has chosen
a different car. I still consider myself an innocent backseat colleague.
The program says that tomorrow she will call Douglas Cardinal 'a
Canadian working at the end of this millennium.' Us too, working hard.
We disembark & are passed by approving soldiers through the hotel
metal detector.

10.

The next morning the pavillion breakfast is served promptly. Our Indian
colleagues are comfortably huddled around the charcoal pots,
speculating about new plots to take over the association. By noon the sun
comes out & our Moslem colleague from Baroda is indeed the new
vice-president. A car bomb has exploded overnight in Srinagar. In
Canada, Indians are plotting to regain treaty rights. A colleague from
Jammu is bringing a car to take us to the maharajah's palace, which is
now an art museum. Quaint watercolours of fierce colonial soldiers.

11.

We return to the hotel. It is late afternoon of New Year's Eve. There are
more soldiers lounging in the lobby. Balloons & streamers newly hang-
ing. The elites of Jammu will soon be here to dance & drink their $700
champagne. Painting bull's eyes on our hotel. Abe & Stan & I share
a bottle of French airline wine behind drawn curtains in my room.
At midnight we hear the traditional explosions & fireworks. Tracer
bullets across the valley. The adventure-book rattle of AK-47s. We take
delight in there being no sound of glass breaking. We shout 'Happy
New Year' collegially.

4. PAR LUI-MÊME

GEORGE BOWERING PAR LUI-MÊME

Has a great jump shot.

Tried his mother's patience.

Was a chaste teen.

Red Sox in 2004!

No, no more chocolate!

Vacuumed Bruce Wayne's mansion.

Home-cooked Ontario lad.

Son of the Okanagan.

Awed by the snow.

Ah! Spring is here!

Remembered Valentine's Day.

Working day and night for Canadian culture.

Favors Truman over Dewey.

Never saw 'Cheers.'

Misses Kellogg's Krumbles.

Rimes with towering.

He's forge powering.

Can blow air out of his eye socket.

And numerous pen names.

Never met John Turner.

Proud Ontarian.

Younger than W.P. Kinsella.

Younger than Audrey Thomas.

Will not live in a tent.

Trying to cope.

Too bashful for this world.

Friend to any enemy of the Yankees.

The prince of early to bed.

Was once a minor character in a Thorne Smith novel.

None of his pen names is hyphenated.

Can really sing 'Oh Danny Boy.'

No longer cuts his toenails in sequence.

Learning to live with one head.

His eyes hurt more than his feet.

Points out the pretty cut flowers at the abattoir.

Straight, no chaser.

Thinks that Uma Thurman is a newcomer.

Who says clothes have to fit?

Oh no!
I sat right on it!

Has twice written about Malacca.

Lives with a groaning dog.

Even my chair is browned off.

Fewer and fewer matching socks.

My headache has a headache.

A present participle and your friend.

Can tie left shoelace.

Does not attend 'Blow-Out' sales.

You call this an equinox?

It's colder in Ottawa.

Liked liver when he was a kid.

Once cooked a bat.

Your friendly present participle.

Lost in the mists of time.

A bum at water polo.

Open to suggestions.

Saw it coming.

Master of Right Reason.

Can't find his Speedo.

Owns fewer and fewer shirts.

Resisting chocolate bars every day.

VIEW FRANK DAVEY'S POETICS

My name is Frank Davey. I am pleased to say I am running for councillor in Ward 1.

Frank Davey summary with 7 pages of lesson plans, quotes, chapter summaries, analysis, encyclopedia entries, essays, research information, and more.

Perhaps Frank Davey's most accessible and memorable book will be his most atypically direct and personal.

View the profiles of professionals named Frank Davey.

View archival description. Fonds MsC 3—Frank Davey fonds. Title and statement of responsibility area. Title proper.

Visit Dr Frank Davey in Mayo County. See contact details, check prices, read reviews, look at pictures, and get directions.

Frank Davey is on Facebook. Join Facebook to connect with Frank Davey and others you may know. Facebook gives people the power.

Frank Davey began his journal of Linda's illness in March, 1999.

We have found 89 people in the UK with the name Frank Davey. Click here to find personal data about Frank Davey including phone numbers, addresses.

Frank Davey first hit the national radar in 1961.

3 Jul 2006—John Harris skewers Canadian academic literary critic Frank Davey.

Frank Davey—Boxer.... Frank Davey. Global ID, 271827. sex, male. division, welterweight.

Frank Davey 1982 graduate of Smithfield High School.

This is our Frank Davey & Co page.

The candidates are Frank Davey, Howard Phee and Tom Vegh.

Watch Frank Davey Videos. Free Streaming Frank Davey Video Clips.

Frank Davey Books. Frank Davey bibliography includes all books by Frank Davey. Book list may include collections, novellas.

Full contact details for Frank Davey Pty Ltd including phone number, map and reviews—TrueLocal.

View Frank Davey's profile and historical records at Ancestry.com.

Find Frank Davey and other long-lost friends at MyLife™. Find Everyone from Your Past.

Visit Amazon.co.uk's Frank Davey Page and shop for all Frank Davey books. Check out pictures, bibliography, biography and community discussions about Frank Davey.

Frank Davey was born Abt. 1870 in England, and died date unknown in Massachusetts.

Get directions to local business, Frank Davey.

Frank Davey and the Firing Squad. Poetics.

But 'Frank Davey' (and I now mark this entity as a subject distinct from the Frank Davey so much an accepted part of Canadian literary history).

Frank Davey...below the excitement of youth, sex, and poetic manifestos.

Dr Frank Davey worked as a Methodist Medical Missionary, at Uzuakoli, from 1936.

Free credit status for FRANK DAVEY LTD (03564645) at IP22 1EA DISS NORFOLK.

Frank Davey's Page on French Language....Norman Frank Davey is now a member of French Language 3.

Find Frank Davey of Cedar Rapids, IA.

1880s Charlotte E. Davey, newspaper proprietor and son Frank Davey printer.

Be the first to comment on payment promptness FRANK DAVEY LTD ...

Frank Davey, partner. Position: I have worked in residential property since I qualified in 1981.

Frank Davey was born in Vancouver, British Columbia, but raised.

Frank Davey talks about the effect on properties of the death watch beetle.

Frank Davey Bricklaying Pty Ltd in Pambula Beach.

The person who was to become the writer Frank Sargeson was born as Norris Frank Davey.

Find more about Frank Davey's biography, profile, cedar rapids, iowa, funeral, ...

Contact details for Frank Davey & Co in Hassocks BN6 9PU from 192.com Business Directory, the best resource for finding Funeral Directors listings.

View a full list of dealers selling art by Frank Davey. Search for galleries that sell Frank Davey art on artnet.

Compare *When Tish Happens* by Frank Davey.

Which authors share a birthday with Frank Davey?—True Knowledge. About Frank Davey. Honest guy seeking the best life has to offer....

Frank Davey (Ontario, Universities) Rate and read about public employees. Find out where and how Canadian tax money is being spent.

Frank Davey was *Tish*, and that *Tish* was and is Frank Davey.

Frank Davey Bricklaying Pty Ltd. (02) 6495 6509. Report this Listing as incorrect.

Stay tuned for a review of Frank Davey's *When Tish Happens*.

Frank Davey & Co Funeral Directors in Hassocks, BN6. Contact them today for more information on their services.

But to this the amount of land Frank Davey owned is still in question.

Frank Davey belongs to the following categories:

Frank Davey writes nasty, vicious lies about me and my dog Boomer.

Watercolor I & II with Frank Davey.

Norris Frank Davey was a homosexual prostitute. Initially he was a hopelessly unsuccessful gay and the first man he hit on (1924) married his sister.

Everything you need to know about Frank Davey.

Who's Dated Who feature on Frank Davey including trivia, quotes, pictures, biography, photos, videos, pics, news, vital stats, fans and facts.

Over thirty years in the making, Frank Davey's careful archaeology of the catalogue of innocence.

Latest News and Information on Frank Davey. Frank Davey, 60, and Daniel Berinson, 41, died when their light plane crashed east of Perth in March last year. The men had been on a joy flight.

Looking for Frank Davey?

Discover Frank Davey.

Frank Davey, a Chartered Surveyor, and his wife Johanne have a passion for houses.

More About the Author. Frank Davey. Discover books, learn about writers, read author blogs, and more.

Free search for Frank Davey—check phone, address, background, criminal records, people finder, public records and...

DAVEY, Frank. Fondest memories of a dear Dad and Grandad, now at rest. Love from Son Clive.

We provide the latest news and info on Frank Davey.

Welcome to the Frank Davey & Co Funeral Home.

At a general election held on the 8th day of November, 1887, GW Wilkinson and Frank Davey each received 697 votes for the office of the treasurer.

Do not forget to check the lastest products and auctions related to Frank Davey as well as our free videos and podcasts.

Frank Davey provides the foundation of Dudek's poetic.

Plaxo helps members like Frank Davey keep in touch with the people who really matter.

Francis John George (Frank) Davey grave monument details. All the legible names shown on the Francis John George (Frank) Davey grave monument.

Fellow co-chairman Frank Davey said Kimberley cultural leaders had said from the start that if the gas project went ahead there would have to be large areas.

Frank Davey has long been a cultural force to be reckoned with.

Frank Davey is associated with Township of Worcester with the role of Chairman. Frank Davey has 4 known relationships.

Frank Davey workin on gas AGAIN. Get qualified or * off to jail.

He didn't last up there long as first it was Stan Coe taking the lead, followed by past-champion Frank Davey taking it over.

Frank DAVEY married Unknown GILL.

Frank Davey located at 2203 Princeton Way Colorado Springs, CO.

Read customer reviews and browse products and services that Frank Davey offers.

What is the summary on poem 'The Piano' by Frank Davey?

Frank Davey : Obituary. Published in the *Sunderland Echo* on 3rd August 2010 (Distributed in Sunderland). This notice has had 111 visitors.

Purchase our Frank Davey Biography Order our Frank Davey Biography ... Ask any question on Frank Davey and get it answered FAST!

Frank Davey 1979 graduate of Jesuit High School in Carmichael, CA is on Memory Lane. Get caught up with Frank and other high school alumni from Jesuit High.

Frank Davey is a leading authority on contemporary Canadian literature and culture.

The practice congratulates Frank Davey FRICS, Consultant Building Surveyor.

Buy *Back To The War* by Frank Davey in India.

View FRANK DAVEY and DONNA ROMBOUSEK event profile on WeddingChannel.com.

Defending track champion Flyin' Frank Davey.

What is the nationality of Frank Davey, the Canadian writer?

F.A. 'Frank' Davey operated the Garnet General Store for 45 years.

To my true friend Frank Davey, in commiseration (if so he will!).

After the Wells Hotel closed in the 1930s, Frank Davey moved into the kitchen.

Last season, Frank Davey finished third in points, which is off of his normal mark.

Buy FRANK DAVEY's books, best sellers, collection. great prices + Free Shipping.

Frank Davey, from New Costessey, pleaded guilty at Norwich Magistrates' Court to breaching health and safety law.

Herbert procured a mini tape recorder from America and gave it to Constable Frank Davey with instructions to secretly tape his co-arresting officers.

Wah says that while attending UBC as a music and English literature major, he met George Bowering and Frank Davey

Now Frank Davey is a driver to keep your eye on.

Report on the Japanese situation in Oregon: investigated for Governor Ben W. Olcott, August, 1920 by Frank Davey.

Frank Davey was a dedicated and aggressive chairman of the Home's board.

Dr. Frank Davey has written: Jesus reversed the social priorities of his day by demonstrating and teaching a special concern for the poor.

One side of the business was a farm machinery dealership run by Mr Rex Davey and the other a successful dairy farm run by Mr Frank Davey OBE.

Frank Davey and Michael Smith. Small right arrow pointing to.

Download: Frank Davey, Dying, Fiction, Autobiography.

Members who intend going to the Branch AGM should contact Frank Davey.

Buy or sell *Popular Narratives* by Frank Davey.

In the case of Frank Davey's sheaf of notes for poems, one responds.

Fact 1: 69 years, 11 months and 24 days old is the age of Frank Davey.

Frank DAVEY founded *Tish* (1961-65) at UBC, stressing the poem as a developing experience, rather than as a finished product.

Frank Davey. Where is Frank these days? I wonder.

Frank Davey treats Anne and shifts in reading of the novel as indices.

Frank Davey: vocal, keyboard, guitar.

Definitions of frank davey, synonyms, antonyms, derivatives of frank davey.

Along with mine, there'll be titles by Frank Davey.

Davey always idolizes other people instead of his own family like gloria and it used to be uncle Frank Davey.

Frank Davey overview and Frank Davey descriptions with footnotes images commentary.

Receive a record of every available piece of public records for Frank Davey—available now from Radaris!

If you like, you can repeat the search with the omitted results included.

THE LETTERS OF MR. O. & MR. C.

I was reading where Mr. Olson writes of 'one R Creeley' and thinking
that he was also a one C Creeley and a three E Creeley

I was reading the letters of Mr. O and Mr. C and there were
a lot of letters often more than fifty on a line

'the trouble with what was done,' Mr. O typed
'(even yesterday), is, today.'

ETHICAL ADVICE ACCUMULATES

It's better to light a candle than to curse the darkness. It is better to give than to take. It is better to travel hopefully than to arrive. It is better to be stung by a nettle than pricked by a rose. It is better to walk than to run in the rain. It is better to be right than be happy.

It is better to buy than to rent. It is better to keep your mouth closed and let people think you are a fool than to open it and remove all doubt. Better to be lowly and have a servant than to play the great man and lack bread. It's better to build boys than mend men. It's better to be single.

It's better to marry than to burn. It's better to divorce than to stay married. It's better to wait than take your pension early. It's better biologically to be of mixed race. It is better to run away from a nuclear fallout than take shelter in a building. It is better to hear the rebuke of the wise than the song of fools.

It's better to be rich. It's better to win a bronze than a silver. 'Tis better to be vile, than vile esteemed. It is better to be hated for what you are than loved for what you are not. It's better to advise and assist than to get involved militarily.

It's better to feel a little too much than not enough. Better to trust in the lord than to put confidence in man. It's better to write than die. Better to be loved than feared. Better to launch a spaceship from near the equator. It is better to go to the house of mourning than to the house of feasting.

It is better to quit than to get fired. Better to leave than surrender. It's better to use an Ethernet connector than a USB. It is better to dwell in a desert than with a contentious and fretful spouse. It's better to kick than to receive.

Better to jump into the game than languish on the sidelines. Better to leave well enough alone. Better to be wrong with Jean-Paul Sartre than right with Raymond Aron. Better to use an online site builder than a stand-alone web editor. Better to travel than to wash grapefruits. Better to be lucky in love than unlucky at lawn bowling.

Better to have a lot of frenemies than no friends at all. Better to die while speaking the truth. Better to get vitamins from food than from supplements. Better to brush your teeth up-and-down than sideways. Better to cheer for the Yanks than boo the Tigers.

Better to have the lyrics and not need them than need them and not have them. Better to burn out than fade away. Better to be Herod's pig than his son. Better to kick ass than to kiss it. Better to leave a glass broken than to cut yourself trying to fix it. Better to look good than feel good.

Better to be frustrated than bored. Better to be lucky than sexy. Better to give more than less. Better to pay down debt than to save. Better to owe taxes than be owed a refund.

Better to die than be killed. Better to be gay than a dictator. Better to have chosen goodness than been born good. It's better to have loved and lost. Better to have problems now than later. Better to be a corporation than an individual.

Better to learn Cantonese than Mandarin. Better to spend your money than let inflation devour it. Better for a woman to pray at home than in a mosque. Better to die in your sleep than know you have six months to live. Better to be safe than sorry.

Better to store bread on the counter than in the fridge. Better to ask forgiveness after than permission before. Better to have Tory loons than Ukip clowns. Better to run alone talking loudly, waving your hands about, as if you are with someone. Better to donate than to accumulate. Better to let the dogs out.

Better to be slapped with the truth than kissed with a lie. Better to be a big fish in a small pond. Better to have a downpayment than a trade-in. Better to be Roger Federer than Alex Rodriguez. Better to reign in hell than serve in heaven.

Better to turn loose five who are guilty than convict one who is innocent. Better to say nothing. Better not to resist than to get injured too. Better to be big and popular than small and niche. Better to be fat and fit than skinny and unfit. Better to bundle than to break it up.

Better to map your reads to genomes than to transcriptomes. Better to do cardio after eating than on an empty stomach. Better to be alone than to be in bad company. Better to protect your community. Better to start from a clean slate than from a dirty one.

Better to smell melted butter than taste a whole cooked cake. Better to go to work for an awesome startup than to go straight to grad school. Better to spend money like there's no tomorrow than to spend tonight like there's no money. Better to give people what they want than what we think they should have. Better to kill a terrorist than call the police. Better to profile than to pat down.

Better to be on disability than work for minimum wage. Better to be short than to be tall and develop cancer. Better to be a binary thinker than to live in continual confusion. Better to be a self-made man than to be half a man, made after some other man's pattern. Better to walk before we run.

Better to be frugal. Better to work than to idle be. Better to settle for less than be alone. Better to be generous than selfish, better to be chaste than licentious, better to be true than false, better to be brave than a coward. Better to keep the schools we have than accept the schools we might have. Better to be an adulterer than a Mormon.

Better to be cool than fat. Better to destroy the country than end the anti-Obamacare drive. Better to teach than to mutilate. Better to keep for a week than a fortnight. Better to be beaten than be in bad company.

Better to settle for less. Better to be an early riser. Tis better thee without than he within. Better to be found than to find. Tis better to sip than to suck. Better to miss the point than miss the channel.

Tis better in the mind to suffer the slings and arrows of outrageous fortune. Tis better to suffer wrong than do it. Tis better to have feared and fled, than never to have feared at all. Tis better to enlarge the mind than expand the wallet. It's better to be righteous than right.

Better to live your own life imperfectly than to imitate someone else's perfectly. Better to have loafed and lost. Tis better to be wise than intelligent. Better to have loved and flossed. Better to give than to lobby. Better to disconnect than stay hard-wired.

Better to walk alone than in a crowd. Better to be seen than not be heard. Better to have rushed and lost. Better to have loved a short person than never loved a tall. Tis better late.

Tis better to give than wait for the tax man. Tis better to have loved and lost than to have paid and messed up. Tis better to recycle than have nothing. Tis better to extend than amend. Tis better to build your fence at the top of the cliff. Tis better to slip with the foot than the tongue.

It's better to pretend you don't know. Better to feed the hog than hog the feed. Better to chance a loss than lose a chance. Better to plant a cabbage than a rose. Tis better to be lowly born than wear a golden sorrow. Better to feed the homeless indoors.

Better to pretend you don't know than to know you're pretending. Better to burn than to look unhealthy. Better to eat the rancid cabbage than feed the raunchy carnivore. Better to have the fish touch the ice than the ice touch the fish.

Better to leave the fluorescent lights on. Better to show than tell. Better to use one condom than two. Better to be told on than tell. Better to raise pokemon from egg. Better green than dead. Better to channel the changes than change the channel. Better to sleep with a sober cannibal than a drunken Christian.

Better Erik the Red than Ethelred the Unred. Better a stitch in time than a cramp in the Tyne. It's better to change the coach than to buy new players. Better to be told on than tell. Better to care too little than to care too much. Better two slices of lemon than one of lime.

ACKNOWLEDGMENTS

Some of these poems have been published in *Rampike* and *Queen Street Quarterly* and in chapbooks published by housepress, above/ground press, and Massassauga.

Frank Davey has been pushing at expanding what poetry can do since helping launch Vancouver's *Tish* poetry newsletter in 1961 and publishing *D-Day and After*—described by James Reaney as appearing to have been written by his typewriter—in 1962. Along the way he has published more than thirty poetry books, most recently *aka bpNichol*, a biography of poet bpNichol, and the artist's book *Spectres of London Ont*. Other books have included *The Abbotsford Guide to India* (1986), winner of the 1987 Canadian Publishers Association Writers Choice Award, *Postcard Translations* (1988) and *Bardy Google* (2010). Frank lives in London, Ontario.

OTHER BOOKS FROM MANSFIELD PRESS

Poetry

Leanne Averbach, *Fever*
Nelson Ball, *In This Thin Rain*
Nelson Ball, *Some Mornings*
Gary Barwin, *Moon Baboon Canoe*
George Bowering, *Teeth: Poems 2006–2011*
Stephen Brockwell, *Complete Surprising Fragments of Improbable Books*
Stephen Brockwell & Stuart Ross, eds., *Rogue Stimulus: The Stephen Harper Holiday Anthology for a Prorogued Parliament*
Diana Fitzgerald Bryden, *Learning Russian*
Alice Burdick, *Flutter*
Alice Burdick, *Holler*
Jason Camlot, *What The World Said*
Margaret Christakos, *wipe.under.a.love*
Pino Coluccio, *First Comes Love*
Marie-Ève Comtois, *My Planet of Kites*
Dani Couture, *YAW*
Gary Michael Dault, *The Milk of Birds*
Frank Davey, *Poems Suitable for Current Material Conditions*
Pier Giorgio Di Cicco, *The Dark Time of Angels*
Pier Giorgio Di Cicco, *Dead Men of the Fifties*
Pier Giorgio Di Cicco, *The Honeymoon Wilderness*
Pier Giorgio Di Cicco, *Living in Paradise*
Pier Giorgio Di Cicco, *Early Works*
Pier Giorgio Di Cicco, *The Visible World*
Salvatore Difalco, *What Happens at Canals*
Christopher Doda, *Aesthetics Lesson*
Christopher Doda, *Among Ruins*
Glenn Downie, *Monkey Soap*
Rishma Dunlop, *The Body of My Garden*
Rishma Dunlop, *Lover Through Departure: New and Selected Poems*
Rishma Dunlop, *Metropolis*
Rishma Dunlop & Priscila Uppal, eds., *Red Silk: An Anthology of South Asian Women Poets*
Ollivier Dyens, *The Profane Earth*
Laura Farina, *Some Talk of Being Human*
Jaime Forsythe, *Sympathy Loophole*
Carole Glasser Langille, *Late in a Slow Time*
Suzanne Hancock, *Another Name for Bridge*
Jason Heroux, *Emergency Hallelujah*
Jason Heroux, *Memoirs of an Alias*
Jason Heroux, *Natural Capital*
John B. Lee, *In the Terrible Weather of Guns*
Jeanette Lynes, *The Aging Cheerleader's Alphabet*
David W. McFadden, *Be Calm, Honey*
David W. McFadden, *Shouting Your Name Down the Well: Tankas and Haiku*
David W. McFadden, *What's the Score?*

Leigh Nash, *Goodbye, Ukulele*
Lillian Necakov, *The Bone Broker*
Lillian Necakov, *Hooligans*
Peter Norman, *At the Gates of the Theme Park*
Peter Norman, *Water Damage*
Natasha Nuhanovic, *Stray Dog Embassy*
Catherine Owen & Joe Rosenblatt, with Karen Moe, *Dog*
Corrado Paina, *The Alphabet of the Traveler*
Corrado Paina, *The Dowry of Education*
Corrado Paina, *Hoarse Legend*
Corrado Paina, *Souls in Plain Clothes*
Stuart Ross et al., *Our Days in Vaudeville*
Matt Santateresa, *A Beggar's Loom*
Matt Santateresa, *Icarus Redux*
Ann Shin, *The Last Thing Standing*
Jim Smith, *Back Off, Assassin! New and Selected Poems*
Jim Smith, *Happy Birthday, Nicanor Parra*
Robert Earl Stewart, *Campfire Radio Rhapsody*
Robert Earl Stewart, *Something Burned on the Southern Border*
Carey Toane, *The Crystal Palace*
Priscila Uppal, *Summer Sport: Poems*
Priscila Uppal, *Winter Sport: Poems*
Steve Venright, *Floors of Enduring Beauty*
Brian Wickers, *Stations of the Lost*

Fiction

Marianne Apostolides, *The Lucky Child*
Sarah Dearing, *The Art of Sufficient Conclusions*
Denis De Klerck, ed., *Particle & Wave: A Mansfield Omnibus of Electro-Magnetic Fiction*
Paula Eisenstein, *Flip Turn*
Sara Heinonen, *Dear Leaves, I Miss You All*
Marko Sijan, *Mongrel*
Tom Walmsley, *Dog Eat Rat*

Non-Fiction

George Bowering, *How I Wrote Certain of My Books*
Rosanna Caira & Tony Aspler, *Buon Appetito Toronto*
Denis De Klerck & Corrado Paina, eds., *College Street–Little Italy: Toronto's Renaissance Strip*
Pier Giorgio Di Cicco, *Municipal Mind: Manifestos for the Creative City*
Amy Lavender Harris, *Imagining Toronto*
David W. McFadden, *Mother Died Last Summer*

To order these books, visit www.mansfieldpress.net